Explanations of Misfortune in the Buddha's Life

The Buddha's Misdeeds in His Former Human Lives and Their Remnants

Stephan Hillyer Levitt

Pariyatti Press

PARIYATTI PRESS
an imprint of
Pariyatti Publishing
www.pariyatti.org

ISBN: 978-1-68172-464-5 (Print)
ISBN: 978-1-68172-465-2 (PDF)
ISBN: 978-1-68172-466-9 (ePub)
ISBN: 978-1-68172-470-6 (Mobi)
Library of Congress Control Number: 2022932653

Special thanks to the Vipassana Research Institute (vridhamma.org) for granting permission to use a Global Vipassana Pagoda (globalpagoda.org) painting by Vasudeo Kamath (vasudeokamath.com) for the cover.

IN MEMORY OF
MY PARENTS,
ABRAHAM AND IDA LEVITT

Preface

Work on the *Detiskarma pardārthayi* began with the help of Dr. Amaradasa Virasinha at the time of its initial cataloguing for the University of Pennsylvania Library in 1973. The text was gone over again with Dr. Virasinha a few years later, after I had located the parallel Pāli text and the relevant commentaries. After another manuscript of the text was located in Sri Lanka, I tried to get a transcription of this but without success. This was tried again in the beginning of 2001 through the offices of the Venerable Pandit Kurunegoda Piyatissa Maha Thera of the New York Buddhist Vihara, again without success.

When J. Liyanaratne 1983 had appeared, however, a third manuscript of the text had been located in the collection of the Bibliothèque Nationale, Paris. This was obtained in microfilm copy in late 2000, and the specific text in question was located in the larger manuscript with the help of the Venerable Piyatissa in the summer of 2001. Also at that time the Venerable Piyatissa went over with me a few of the questions I had regarding the Pāli text, and went over a few sections of the Paris manuscript with me. A Xerox copy of the microfilm of the Bibliothèque Nationale, Paris manuscript was forwarded, though, through the good offices of Dr. Amaradasa Virasinha (now retired from the University of Pennsylvania Library and living in Sri Lanka) to Dr. Jinadasa Liyanaratne (Associate Professor in Sinhala at the Institut National des Langues et Civilisations Orientales in Paris) in the spring of 2002 for him to go over this manuscript.

The Pāli text was gone over again in full with the Venerable Piyatissa in the summer of 2004.

The help of both Dr. Amaradasa Virasinha and Dr. Jinadasa Liyanaratne with this text has been invaluable. Thanks are in order to Dr. Jinadasa Liyanaratne for his valuable suggestions and comments. And, without question, the Venerable Piyatissa is also to be greatly thanked for his help.

In addition, thanks must go to Bob Scott, head of Columbia University Library's Electronic Text Service for his help with the computer editions of the *Tipiṭaka* and its commentaries.

And thanks must go to the Buddhist Literature Society, Inc. and the Corporate Body of the Buddha Educational Foundation for their invaluable gift of *dhamma* (*dhammadāna*) in publishing this work.

The Sinhalese text of the *Detiskarmmay* from the Bibliotheque Nationale, Paris was translated by Dr. Jinadasa Liyanaratne. Dr. Amaradasa Virasinha translated the University of Pennsylvania Sinhalese text of the *Detiskarma padarthayi.*

Stephan Hillyer Levitt
Flushing, New York
U. S. A.
June, 2009

Table of Contents

Introduction

There is housed in the University of Pennsylvania Museum Indic and Greater Indic manuscript collection (currently housed together with the Indic manuscript collection of the Library of the University of Pennsylvania) a manuscript of a text in Pāli and Sinhalese called the *Detiskarma padārthayi.*[1] This text proves to be the *Pubbakammapiloti* of the *Apadāna* of the *Khuddaka Nikāya* (hence, *Pkp*), which treats the misdeeds of the Buddha in his former human lives, plus a few extra verses in Pāli, a word-for-word translation into Sinhalese, a Sinhalese retelling of the verses, and several additional stories in Sinhalese treating the same topic. The additional stories bring the number of *kamma*s treated to seventeen. *UP* has many misspellings. The Sinhalese retellings, though, prove to be much fuller than the Pāli verses.

In this text, the Buddha explains that all deeds have their consequences, even for him and even in his life as the Buddha. In a sense, this responds to the problem of the righteous sufferer with which Ancient Mesopotamian religion grappled from the middle of the second millenium BCE. It is a Buddhist treatment of the questions raised in the Old Testament Book of Job (probably no earlier than the 5th c. BCE, perhaps 4th c. BCE). I have argued elsewhere that the concept of *kamma* (Skt. *karma*) is a response to this ancient Mesopotamian problem, in India.[2]

Interestingly, none of the bad deeds were done in animal lives. This probably reflects the Indian belief that animals act according to their *svabhāva*, or "innate nature", as for example in the *Hitopadeśa* and the *Pañcatantra*. Thus a jackal is

1. For a cataloguing of this manuscript (hence, *UP*) see S. H. Levitt, 1980, p. 134.
2. See S. H. Levitt, 2003, pp. 352b, 354b.

a wily scoundrel, a fish is thoughtful, a cat is a hypocrite and remorseless, and so forth. While there is latitude regarding one's behaviour in accord with one's *svabhāva*, as in the *Mitacintijātaka* in which we have three fish, "Thinking-Little", "Thinking-Too-Much", and "Proper-Thinking", the implication is that one does not thereby obtain bad *kamma*.[3] Even if one does outright bad deeds, as the jackal in the *Biḷārajātaka* or the four cats in the *Babbujātaka*, the implication is that one does not obtain bad *kamma* if one acts in accord with one's *svabhāva*.[4] *Bhagavadgītā* 18, 40-48 implies on the other hand that humans can act other than in accord with their *svabhāva*, or nature.

In short, there is a general attitude in Indian belief that if one acts according to one's *svabhāva* or acts in accord with one's *dharma*, there is no bad merit accrued.[5] Franklin Edgerton's translation of the *Bhagavadgītā* 18, 40-41 and 47 states:

> 40. There is no thing, whether on earth,
> Or yet in heaven, among the gods,
> No being which free from the material-nature-born
> Strands, these three, might be.
>
> 41. Of brahmans, warriors, and artisans,
> And of serfs, scorcher of the foe,
> The actions are distinguished
> According to the Strands that spring from their innate nature.
>
> 47. Better one's own duty, (even) imperfect,
> Than another's duty well performed.
> Action pertaining to his own estate
> Performing, he incurs no guilt.

---

3. See *J*, vol. 1, pp. 426-28 (*Jātaka* no. 114) and *SBFB*, vol. 1, pp. 256-57 for this *Jātaka*.
4. For the *Biḷārajātaka* see *J*, vol. 1, pp. 460-61 (*Jātaka* no. 128) and *SBFB*, vol. 1, pp. 281-82. For the *Babbujātaka*, see *J*, vol. 1, pp. 477-80 (*Jātaka* no. 137) and *SBFB*, vol. 1, pp. 294-96.
5. The *Bhagavadgītā* further emphasizes action without attachment to results as leading to salvation.

See also Annie Besant's translation, which is particularly clear on this point.

Carrying this line of thought further, we have in Indian tradition belief in an "act of truth" (Pāli *saccakiriyā*, Sanskrit **satyakriyā*), which one can obtain the ability to perform by doing one's *dharma*, or "duty" perfectly, even if one is a prostitute, for instance, as in *Milindapañha* 4, 1, 47.[6]

In later Buddhist philosophy, Nāgārjuna denies the existence of *svabhāva*.[7] Also, in the *Pitṛputrasamāgama*, *Sikṣāsamuccaya* of later Buddhism, it is stated that in an illusory world *karma* is also illusory.[8]

There is also indication in the Pāli literature that one's *svabhāva* as an animal continues in one's human life. Thus, for example, the first *Sigālajātaka* states that Devadatta's lying nature today is the same as when he was a jackal in a previous life.[9] On the other hand, in the third *Sigālajātaka*, the Bodhisatta is a jackal but he learns by his behaviour not to be greedy. "Once bitten, twice shy."[10]

Also interesting, the bad events in the Buddha's life which are attributed to *kamma* flow naturally from circumstances mentioned with regard to these incidents elsewhere in the Pāli canon. Thus, the slander of Ciñca-mānavikā can be attributed

---

6. Regarding this latter point, see E. W. Burlingame, 1917, pp. 439-41 and W. Norman Brown, 1940-41, p. 37, 1972, pp. 256-57 (Rpt., 1978, p. 107). For a bibliography on the "act of truth" see W. Norman Brown, 1972, p. 252, n. 1 (Rpt., 1978, p. 102, n. 1).

7. See Nāgārjuna's *Mūlamadhyamakārikā* 1, 1-14 as in Jay L. Garfield, 1995, pp. 3-5 (Garfield's commentary, pp. 103-25), the introduction to Jay L. Garfield's commentary in this volume, p. 89 and n. 4, and the *Mahāyāna Viṃśaka*, or "Twenty Verses of the Great Vehicle" in Susumu Yamaguchi, 1927, pp. 169-71 (Rpt., 1957, pp. 338-39). The latter states, "The self-nature of all things is regarded as like shadows; they are in substance pure, serene, non-dualistic, and same as suchness."

8. See A. L. Basham, 1958, pp. 178-79. The *Sikṣāsamuccaya* was compiled by Śāntideva in the 7th c. CE.

9. See *J*, vol. 1, pp. 424-26 (*Jātaka* no. 113) and *SBFB*, vol. 1, pp. 255-56.

10. See *J*, vol. 1, pp. 501-504 (*Jātaka* no. 148) and *SBFB*, vol. 1, pp. 314-16 (quote, p. 316).

to her having been a member of a heretical ascetic order which found that their gains had grown less due to the popularity of the Buddha. The enmity of Māgandiyā is also due to the Buddha's having referred to her as a "vessel of filth" when he rejected her father's offer of her hand in marriage. The active enmity of Devadatta is due to his jealousy of Buddha encouraged by his successs in winning over Ajātasattu to his side. The Buddha's bodily aches and pains can be attributed to his having undergone severe self-mortification for six years.[11] Thus, from the vantage of the Buddhist tradition as a whole, events flow naturally from every day causality as well as *kamma.*

The manuscript catalogues list only two other manuscripts with the title under consideration. One, in Sri Lanka, is in Śastrāravinda Pirivin Vihāraya, Polgolla, Gokarälla.[12] The other, in the Bibliothèque Nationale, Paris refers to itself as *Detiskarmmaya.*[13] I have been unable to get a transcription of the manuscript in Sri Lanka (see Preface), but have obtained film of the manuscript in the Bibliothèque Nationale, Paris (hence, *BN*). While this is also a Sinhalese retelling of *Pkp*, it does not contain the Pāli verses as such after the first few verses, providing in general only a few Pāli citations at random at the beginnings of the sections of Sinhalese text, sometimes citing only the first word of the Pāli text. In the beginning of the text some Pāli words are explained in Sinhalese, but this is the exception. On the whole this manuscript is not a *sanne* proper as is *UP* in that a word-for-word Sinhalese translation is not given. This is all certainly the reason why it refers to itself as *Detiskarmmaya* instead of *Detiskarma padārthayi.* Also, in *BN* additional *kammas* are added, bringing their total to twenty-two. Some of the additional *kammas* are the same as in *UP*, though one of the additional *kammas* in *UP* is not found

11. This latter explanation is given by *DPPN*, vol. 2, p. 618 in the course of the discussion of Māra.

12. This is listed in K. D. Somadasa, 1959-64 under the title, *Detiskarma padārthayi.*

13. See J. Liyanaratne, 1983, p. 53, Ms. no. 6 (Smith-Lesouf 269), text no. 68.

here. However, there is a corresponding *kamma* instead. On the whole, the Sinhalese text in *UP* and in *BN* correspond well to one another, though *UP* is perhaps more corrupt. The primary purpose of the present volume is to present the *UP* and *BN* to the scholarly community, as well as those who have a general interest in Buddhism.

The *Apadāna* and the *Pubbakammapiloti* (*Pkp*)

The larger text in which *Pkp* is found, the *Apadāna*, is said to be the thirteenth book of the *Khuddaka Nikāya* of the *Sutta Piṭaka* according to Buddhaghosa, but there are conflicting views regarding this arrangement.[14] The book consists of four main sections, the *Buddhāpadāna*, the *Paccekabuddhāpadāna*, the *Therāpadāna*, and the *Therīapadāna*. These four sections are divided into fifty-nine groups. Of them, the first fifty-five consist of 550 tales about *theras*, each group consisting of ten tales. In the first group are also included the *Buddhāpadāna* and the *Paccekabuddhāpadāna* which are but minor sections of the book. The last four groups of the book consist of forty tales of *therīs*, each group consisting of ten tales.[15] S. M. Cutler reports that there is variability as to the actual number of *apadānas* of the *theras*, most manuscripts containing a total of 547. There is also evidence of an additional eleven *apadānas* which are not included in most editions of the text. It would seem that there has been a conscious effort on the part of the redactor to match the number of these stories to the number of *jātakas* in the *Jātaka* collection.[16]

The *Buddhāpadāna* departs from the general pattern maintained in the *Therāpadāna* and *Therīapadāna*. In this section, the Buddha tells of ideal lands of beauty where the Buddhas live. A picture is painted of Buddhas questioning each other, and there is mention of disciples questioning the Buddhas and vice versa. Furthermore, the presentation of the

---

14. See S. M. Cutler, 1994, p. 2 and pp. 20-21.
15. See H. R. Perera, 1966, p. 26.
16. S. M. Cutler, 1994, pp. 36-37.

karmic connection between the particular pious deed of the Bodhisatta which it describes, a mental rather than a physical offering done at a time when the Bodhisatta was close to the end of his path toward Buddhahood, and its fruit, the attainment of enlightenment, is so understated that it has not always been noticed.[17] K. R. Norman, in fact, states that "the *Buddhāpadāna* in its present form lacks the essential feature of an *apadāna*: it says nothing about the Buddha's previous existences, and seems more like an *udāna* than an *apadāna*."[18] The mention of numerous Buddhas and of ideal lands of beauty where the Buddhas live give evidence to a very late date for this section of the *Apadāna*.[19]

The *Paccekabuddhāpadāna*, despite its place in the collection, is not truly an *apadāna* and its inclusion is anomalous. It is recited by the Buddha in response to a request by Ānanda for information about the *paccekabuddhas*. In the course of his reply, the Buddha quotes the whole of the *Khaggavisāṇa Sutta*, the Rhinocerous *Sutta*, of the *Sutta Nipāta*. There is no indication in this *sutta* itself that the verses are to be connected with *paccekabuddhas* although the *Culla Niddesa* attributes them to the *paccekabuddhas*, as does the *Mahāvastu*. Even though the introductory verses here are almost identical to those of the *Buddhāpadāna*, this cannot disguise the fact that the *Paccekabuddhāpadāna* was deliberately composed around the verses of another canonical work in order to complete the creation of a formal structure for the *Apadāna* collection.[20]

The main portion of the work, the *Therāpadānas* and *Therīapadānas*, is a collection of legends in verse in which the noble deeds done by the Buddhist *theras* and *therīs* in earlier existences are glorified. The *Apadāna* is almost an appendix to the *Theragāthā* and *Therīgāthā*, and many of the authors of the *apadānas* are also mentioned in the *Theragāthā* and *Therīgāthā*.

17. See S. M. Cutler, 1994, pp. 7-8 and pp. 12-13.
18. K. R. Norman, 1983, p. 91.
19. H. R. Perera, 1966, p. 3a; K. R. Norman, 1983, pp. 90-91.
20. H. R. Perera, 1966, p. 2b; K. R. Norman, 1983, p. 91; S. M. Cutler, 1994, pp. 10-11.

The *Apadāna* collection, however, includes many *thera*s who do not appear in the *Theragāthā*, and does not include all the *therī*s in the *Therīgāthā*. The *Apadāna* does include, however, at least one *therī* for whom there is no poem in the *Therīgāthā*, Yasodharā. Also, the poems of the *Thera* and *Therīgāthā*s are arranged like those of the *Jātaka*, according to the number of verses they contain, and a wide range of metres are represented. A numerical system of arrangement is not followed in the *Apadāna* and it is composed entirely in *śloka* metre, with the exception of the first three verses of the *Buddhāpadāna* and the whole of the *Paccekabuddhāpadāna* which are in *triṣṭubh* metre. These *Apadāna* narratives of the Buddhist *thera*s and *therī*s display both lateness and the influence of the popular and lay sphere since, instead of explaining the winning of holiness through the practices of the eightfold path, the monks and nuns seek the cause for it in pious actions which they performed in their previous existences by offering flowers, water, fruit, and fans to the Buddhas of the past who gave them in return a prophesy that they would hear the doctrine of Gotama Buddha. The stories go on to say how this came true, and how the authors became *arahant*s. There is mention here of the worship of *thūpa*s, shrines, and relics, and there is an emphasis on generosity and humanitarian deeds.[21]

At the end of the *Therāpadāna* there is placed the *Pkp*, our text here, which disjunctively figures itself to be a *Buddhāpadāna* along with the earlier *Buddhāpadāna* placed at the beginning of the collection. It is one of three texts in the *Apadāna* to be spoken by the Buddha.[22] This is not the only text in the collection which treats the effects of bad or evil deeds. See, for instance, the *Upālittherāpadāna*. As S. M. Cutler points out, "the *apadāna* genre does not deal solely with noble or glorious deeds and their fruit and may also deal with the effects of bad or evil deeds when this is necessary for the provision of

---

21. H. R. Perera, 1966, pp. 2b-3a; K. R. Norman, 1983, pp. 90-91; É. Lamotte, 1988, pp. 691-92.
22. See S. M. Cutler, 1994, p. 11 and pp. 14-15.

a complete karmic explanation of an individual's biography."[23] Such treatment of bad *kamma* in the *Apadāna*, though, is rare.

As noted above, there is evidence in the manuscripts of variability as to the number of *Therāpadānas*, and the number may have been juggled to achieve 547 so as to match the number of *jātakas*. There is also suggestion that the *Paccekabuddhāpadāna* was inserted so as to achieve the threefold ideal grouping of *sāvaka*, *paccekabuddha*, and *sammāsambuddha* which characterizes all the Śrāvakayāna schools including the Theravāda. S. M. Cutler points out that it is obvious that the *Paccekabuddhāpadāna* was specifically composed in response to the demand that the structure of the *Apadāna* reflect this threefold ideal.[24] K. R. Norman draws attention to the fact that mainland Prakrit features not found in Pāli are found in the *Apadāna*, one such feature being particularly associated with the *Buddhāpadana*.[25] Thus both linguistic evidence and content suggest the *Buddhāpadana* is very late. And further it does not fit well with the main portion of the *Apadāna* collection. Still further, the placement of *Pkp* at the end of the *Therāpadāna*, as it is placed in the Buddhist Sanskrit *Anavataptagāthā*, and its placement after the *apadāna* for the elder monk Soṇa-Koṭivīsa the parallel Buddhist Sanskrit text from the *Anavataptagāthā* with which it agrees word-for-word, shows modelling of this text in part on the *Anavataptagāthā* or some similar text. The Sarvāstivādin *Anavataptagāthā* becomes transferred to the *Bhaiṣajyavastu* of the *Mūlasarvāstivāda Vinaya* as the *Sthaviragāthā*, or *Pañcaśatasthavirāvadāna*, "Deeds of the Five Hundred Elders." Also note, the recitation of both the Pāli and Buddhist Sanskrit texts are placed at lake Anotatta (Skt. Anavatapta).[26] The problem posed by the placement of *Pkp* which describes itself as a *Buddhāpadāna* fades in this context. It is not to de-emphasize it as both J. S. Walters and S. M.

23. S. M. Cutler, 1994, pp. 12-13.
24. S. M. Cutler, 1994, p. 27.
25. K. R. Norman, 1983, pp. 91-92.
26. Nalinaksha Dutt, 1947, pp. 20-28; Marcel Hofinger, 1954, pp. 22-23; Heinz Bechert, 1958, pp. 10-13, 1961-65, p. 797ab; *AS*, pp. 29-30.

Cutler have suggested in passing.[27] *Pkp* is not included so as to enable the *Buddhāpadāna* spoken earlier and which is very unlike an *apadāna* to be more like an *apadāna*, as suggested by K. R. Norman.[28] Rather, we have a composite text consciously edited to conform to various criteria. As S. M. Cutler notes, "the problematic features of the *Apadāna* collection are a result of its composite nature, and reflect the changes and developments in Buddhism in the centuries between the death of the Buddha and the writing down of the Theravādin canon."[29]

S. M. Cutler points out that texts such as the *Apadāna* were intended to be used by monks and nuns in their role as preachers and transmitters of the Buddhist doctrine. They were thus directed particularly toward lay audiences. It would appear, though, that at a relatively early date the *Apadāna* declined in popularity as a preaching text, although parts of it continued to be quoted and used as the basis of stories in prose anthologies.[30] "Its homilectic function was apparently taken over by prose narratives such as those of the *Pūjāvaliya*, a thirteenth century collection of stories in Sinhala some of which contain quotes from the *Apadāna* itself."[31] It was also such homilectic function which no doubt was the intention of our text here, the *Detiskarma padārthayi* and *Detiskarmmaya*. Further, as S. M. Cutler has noted, the versions of the *Apadāna* which are available to us show that we possess a corrupt and late redaction of the text.[32]

The first person to notice the similarity between *Pkp* and the comparable text in the *Dul-ba* of the Tibetan *Kanjur* was Léon Feer.[33] Nalinaksha Dutt thinks the Pāli *Apadāna* collection and the *Sthaviragāthā* of the *Mūlasarvāstivāda Vinaya* have a common source. He points to the word-for-

27. J. S. Walters, 1990, p. 92, n. 13; S. M. Cutler, 1994, p. 14.
28. K. R. Norman, 1983, p. 91.
29. S. M. Cutler, 1994, p. 38.
30. S. M. Cutler, 1994, pp. 34-35.
31. S. M. Cutler, 1994, p. 35.
32. S. M. Cutler, 1994, p. 36.
33. Léon Feer, 1897, pp. 292-93.

word similarity between the Pāli and Sanskrit versions of the *apadāna* attributed to Soṇa-Koṭivīsa (Skt. Koṭīviṃśa), and the similarity of *Pkp* to the Tibetan translation of the various verses of the corresponding Sanskrit original. This portion of the Buddhist Sanskrit Gilgit manuscripts was missing. He notes, though, that he finds only occasional agreements between the biographical references in the *Apadāna*, the *Theragāthā*, and the *Sthaviragāthā*.[34] Marcel Hofinger follows upon this with the opinion that the Pāli *Apadāna* collection has a source in the Sanskrit Hīnayāna tradition.[35] Heinz Bechert opines that on the basis of the literal similarity between the Pāli and Buddhist Sanskrit stories of Soṇa-Koṭivīsa, the placement of the Pāli story of Soṇa-Koṭivīsa to immediately precede *Pkp* in the Pāli *Apadāna* collection, the placement of *Pkp* at the end of the *Apadāna* stories of the *theras* just as it appears at the end of the *Anavataptagāthā*'s stories of the elders, and on the basis of the number of similar *theras* of whom stories are told in both collections, the Pāli *Apadāna* collection is based on a recension of the *Anavataptagāthā* not unlike that in the *Bhaiṣajyavastu* of the *Mūlasarvāstivāda Vinaya*.[36] K. R. Norman opines that the *Apadāna* tradition, while the text as we have it is probably late, must be very old and must be the common property of different Hīnayāna schools of Buddhism.[37] To be noted is that the *Anavataptagāthā* version of *Pkp* speaks of only ten *kammas*, whereas the standard Pāli text refers to twelve.

J. S. Walters, treating only *Pkp*, argues that *Pkp* has its origin in a Hīnayāna tradition other than the Theravāda, *e.g.* the Sarvāstivāda or Mahāsaṅghika.[38] Firstly, the term *kammapiloti* is not used anywhere in the Pāli canon and commentaries except in reference to this text. The *Divyāvadāna* of the Sarvāstivādins, however, uses the Sanskrit equivalent *karmaploti* quite often, he

34. Nalinaksha Dutt, 1947, pp. 20-28.
35. Marcel Hofinger, 1954, pp. 22-23.
36. Heinz Bechert, 1958, pp. 10-13, 1961-65, p. 797ab; *AS*, pp. 29-30.
37. K. R. Norman, 1983, p. 92.
38. J. S. Walters, 1990, pp. 77-79.

argues, usually in a stereotyped phrase.[39] The term is also used often in the *Avadānaśataka*.[40] And the Sarvāstivādins seem to have known the prototype of the text. "The *Divyâvadâna*, in the midst of a catalogue of the places where the Buddha made especially important disclosures, states that 'the previous strands of karma have been disclosed at the Great Lake Anavatapta [by the Buddha who was] with the disciples'."[41] Another clue, he argues, points to the Mahāsaṅghikas. Only one of the stories of previous lives has an antecedent in the Pāli texts, namely the story of Jotipāla and Kassapa, in a telling which does not suggest that the Bodhisatta slandered that Buddha or produced bad *kamma* thereby. The majority of the stories about the Buddha's evil deeds in earlier lives are unique to *Pkp*. But the Mahāsaṅghika *Mahāvastu-avadāna* records one of the "unknown" stories, namely the slander by the Bodhisatta of a disciple of the Buddha Sarvābhibhū (P. Sabbābhibhū). This description is considerably more detailed than the mere reference to this event in *Pkp*. It is especially significant since it also parallels the Pāli text in describing the slander of the Buddha by a woman (whose name is lost in a textual lacuna) as a karmic effect of the Buddha's earlier deed.[42] We can also note that in the Gilgit manuscripts, in a section prior to the *Sthaviragāthā*, a story is given parallel to that of the Buddha having had to eat barley for three months in Verajjā as told in *Pkp*. Just as the *Apadāna* story is related to the Buddha in a previous birth having cast aspersions on the Buddha Phussa and his disciples, so here also the parallel story is related to the Buddha in a previous life having cast aspersions on Vipaśyi Buddha and his disciples saying that they deserved only barley grains and not the good food offered by the faithful.[43]

---

39. See *Divy*, p. 87, l. 8; p. 150, l. 24; p. 241, ll. 25-26 (listed in Walters as l. 26).
40. See *Av-ś*, p. 242, l. 9; p. 246, l. 11 (misprinted in Walters as l. 9); p. 249, l. 12 (misprinted in Walters as l. 13); p. 253, l. 6; p. 257, l. 8; p. 267, l. 14; p. 275, l. 12.
41. J. S. Walters, 1990, p. 78.
42. See J. J. Jones, 1949-56, vol. 1, pp. 29-39.
43. See Nalinaksha Dutt, 1947, pp. 4-5.

The weight of the evidence to date would seem to indicate that the tradition of *Pkp* developed in the Sanskrit Hīnayāna tradition, but was then expanded in the Pāli tradition, and further expanded in the Sinhalese Buddhist tradition.

The location of the *Anavataptagāthā* as included in the *Bhaiṣajyavastu* of the *Mūlasarvāstivāda Vinaya* in Tibetan translation is given by Heinz Bechert.[44] The text of the Tibetan verses parallel to the Pāli verses in *Pkp* and their location in the *Dul-ba* of the Tibetan *Kanjur* is given by Nalinaksha Dutt.[45] The text of the entire Tibetan section comparable to the Pāli *Pkp* and its location is given in *AS*.[46] A German translation of the Tibetan text is also given in *AS*.[47]

The location of the *Anavataptagāthā* as included in the *Bhaiṣajyavastu* of the *Mūlasarvāstivāda Vinaya* in Chinese translation is given by Heinz Bechert.[48] The text of the *Anavataptagāthā* here is incomplete, and does not include the parallel text to *Pkp*.[49] An independent translation of the *Anavataptagāthā* is available as well.[50] This contains text parallel to *Pkp*.[51] It is translated into German in *AS*.[52] Another Chinese text which contains material parallel to *Pkp* can also be found.[53] This contains the verses of the Buddha which were inserted at one time between an accompanying account in prose. A German translation of the verses is also given in *AS*.[54]

---

44. Heinz Bechert, 1961-65, p. 796b; *AS*, p. 12.
45. Nalinaksha Dutt, 1947, pp. 22-28.
46. *AS*, pp. 204-243.
47. *AS*, pp. 244-48.
48. Heinz Bechert, 1961-65, p. 796b; *AS*, p. 13. The text is *Taishō* no. 1448, vol. 24, pp. 78a-94a. The entire text of *Taishō* no. 1448 extends from vol. 24, pp. 1a-97a.
49. See Heinz Bechert, 1961-65, p. 796b; *AS*, p. 206 and p. 208.
50. *Taishō* no. 199, vol. 4, pp. 190a-202a. See Heinz Bechert, 1961-65, p. 797a; *AS*, p. 13.
51. See *Taishō* no. 199, vol. 4, pp. 201b, l. 13-202a, l. 14.
52. *AS*, pp. 208-243.
53. See *Taishō* no. 197, vol. 4, pp. 163c-174b.
54. *AS*, pp. 208-243.

The Buddhist Sanskrit text corresponding to *Pkp* is lacking in the *Sthaviragāthā* as in the Gilgit manuscripts.[55] The Gilgit manuscripts, though, do contain part of a prose repetition of the verses spoken by the Buddha, with leaves containing the account missing at both beginning and end.[56] Only a very few partly preserved verses remain toward the end of the Sanskrit version of *Pkp* in the *Anavataptagāthā* as in the Turfan manuscripts.[57] The recently acquired British Library *kharoṣṭhī* birch bark scroll fragments from Gandhāra and the more recently reported Senior collection of Gandhāran Buddhist birch barck scrolls and scroll fragments also both contain sections of text corresponding to the *Anavataptagāthā*, but neither contains the end of the text in which the text corresponding to *Pkp* is to be found.[58]

With regard to *Pkp*, J. S. Walters points to a disagreement in Theravāda Buddhist tradition regarding whether or not the Buddha's sufferings were due to bad *kamma*.[59] He notes that the *Milindapañha* Dilemmas generally affirm the *Apadāna* position that even spiritually advanced people might suffer because of bad *kamma*, but in one such Dilemma it passes on the opportunity to note that the Bodhisatta, along with Devadatta, also obtained bad *kamma* in previous lives. Similarly, in Dilemmas 45 and 46 it denies that the Bodhisatta accumulated bad *kamma* when he slaughtered animals for sacrifice and when he reviled the Buddha Kassapa, respectively. The former is attributed to the acts of a man temporarily insane and therefore not productive of bad *kamma*; the latter was due to the Bodhisatta's Brahman birth and family surroundings. While the demerit gained from slaughtering animals is not included in *Pkp*, it is only in the *Apadāna* that the story of reviling Kassapa is told to exemplify the Buddha's bad *kamma*. "The *Milindapañha* admits the story,

---

55. Nalinaksha Dutt, 1947, pp. 21-22.
56. Nalinaksha Dutt, 1947, pp. 28-29.
57. *AS*, p. 208, p. 239, p. 241.
58. See Richard Salomon, 1999, pp. 30-33, p. 43, pp. 138-39, 2003, p. 79, p. 80.
59. J. S. Walters, 1990, pp. 79-90.

but denies that it was a *karma*producing event."[60] In Dilemma 8, Nāgasena specifically says that the Buddha had burnt out all evil in himself when he became Buddha. Then Milinda asks whether the Buddha suffered bodily pain and Nāgasena answers in the affirmative. Milinda argues that since all pain is the result of *kamma*, the Buddha must have had residual bad *kamma*. Nāgasena, though, cites a passage in the *Saṃyutta Nikāya* in which the Buddha says that not all bodily pain is caused by *kamma*, and argues that the pain suffered by the Buddha was due to natural causes. In Dilemma 26 which concerns the rock hurled by Devadatta which splintered and injured the Buddha's foot, the *Milindapañha* again argues natural causes.

The *Dhammapadaṭṭhakathā* retells several of the stories of unpleasant events in the Buddha's biography without any hint that the Buddha's own bad *kamma* was involved. Thus Sundarī's slander of the Buddha was caused by the jealousy of heretics. Regarding the cycle of stories about Devadatta in the *Apadāna* account, it portrays Devadatta as the causal agent of the Buddha's suffering and shifts the focus to Devadatta's own bad *kamma*. The Buddha and the monks being forced to eat inferior food in Verajjā, it argues, was the result of the bad *kamma* accumulated by the monks during one of the Buddha's previous lives.

Similarly, the *Jātakaṭṭhakathā* also retells the stories of times in which the Buddha suffered seemingly in order to refute the karmic explanation.

The texts which deny the karmic explanation of the Buddha's sufferings never mention *Pkp*, as though it did not exist. But their arguments clearly speak to the problems it raises.

Since *Pkp* is included in the canon as authentically promulgated by the Buddha himself, according to the canon the Buddha himself sided with those Buddhists favoring a karmic explanation for his sufferings. While the arguments of those favoring a karmic explanation never mention the denials of their position specifically, the manner in which they elaborate

60. J. S. Walters, 1990, p. 81.

on the simple *Pkp* references makes clear, according to J. S. Walters, that they are writing with these denials in mind.

The earliest such text is the *Paramattha-Dīpanī Udānaṭṭhakathā* of Dhammapālācariya, his commentary to the *Udāna*. It is the *Udāna* which is the earliest canonical text to tell the story of Sundarī the slanderer. Here Dhammapāla cites by name the *Apadāna* and proceeds to quote *Pkp* in its entirety. Dhammapāla refers his account to a debate over the cause for Sundarī's slander, and states that even though he was Buddha, with all the merit described by the *Jātakas*, still the Buddha was subject to the effects of his previous bad deeds.

One subtradition in the transmission of the *Dhammapadaṭṭhakathā*, which the Pali Text Society edition labelled "Kambodian", did not like the implications of its silence with regard to the Buddha's bad *kamma* apparently. It appends to the *Dhammapadaṭṭhakathā* account of the Ciñca-mānavikā slander a statement that this was due to the Buddha's previous *kamma*. The text then gives the account of the Buddha's birth as Munāli, apparently quoting from the *Apadānaṭṭhakathā*, and then quotes the verses of *Pkp* regarding Ciñca-mānavikā, concluding "this is the former *kamma* of the Master".

The quintessential rebuttal to the denials the Buddha had bad *kamma* is the commentary on *Pkp* contained in the *Visuddhajanavilāsinī nāma Apadānaṭṭhakathā*. *Pkp* receives more attention from the commentator than any other text of the large *Apadāna* collection. The commentary contains lengthy descriptions of the previous life stores, the intermediate sufferings in hell and low states, and the stories of the Buddha's sufferings in this life. In the process of this elaboration, the commentator is able to undercut the denials of the karmic explanations.

The ways in which the commentator does this are interesting. First, the order in which the stories are told is changed, so that the commentary is chronological in terms of Buddha's present life. That is, the six years' asceticism is told first, not last as in *Pkp*, because it preceded all the other unpleasant events chronologically. In the process of narrating these events chronologically, the commentator demonstrates that as the Bodhisatta neared his goal, and even after the great events in his life as Buddha, he continued to suffer bad *kamma*. Second, the commentary addresses the nature of "badness" of the Buddha's *kamma*. In the commentary, less significant deeds like the happy mind of the fisherboy when he sees fish being heaped up and dying are categorized as *akusalakamma*, "unwholesome *kamma*", whereas the major offences like murdering his own half brother and greed are described as *pāpakamma*, "evil *kamma*". Third, the commentator sometimes deepens the karmic connection by providing previous *kamma* explanations for the evil deeds done in the past. Thus when Jotipāla slandered the Buddha Kassapa the primary karmic force which brought it about was Kassapa's own previous bad *kamma*. Fourth, the commentator provides previous bad *kamma* explanations for the alternate causalities propounded by the texts that denied the Buddha suffered the effects of bad *kamma*. Thus Devadatta's enmity, which the *Milindapañha* and other texts state to be the real cause of the Buddha's suffering at his hand, is in the commentary explained to be itself the result of Buddha, in a former life as a merchant, having cheated Devadatta of his due. Fifth, the commentator treats *Pkp* at the beginning of the *Apadāna*, as part of the *Buddhāpadāna* section of the text. For him, the stories about bad *kamma* and bad effects are part of the same story which tells good *kamma* and good effects. The Buddha biography is not only paradigmatic of the pleasant and ultimately liberating effects of good *kamma*. It is also paradigmatic of every person's ability to get onto the right road, even if he or she be a doer of bad *kamma*.

Last to be considered by J. S. Walters is the *ṭīkā* on the *Milindapañha*, a late medieval text which originated in a Sinhalese Mahāvihāra monastery in Thailand. The commentator does not agree with the stand taken by the *Milindapañha* in this debate. The commentator upholds the *Pkp* position that even Buddhas must experience the effects of unrealized bad *kamma*. Even as Buddha, the Buddha had to finish burning up his *kamma*. But being Buddha, this left no residue for rebirth.

Thus the author of this commentary postulates a kind of *kamma* which is only experienced and which results in no further *kamma*. The Buddha experienced bad *kamma*, but it wasn't the kind of *kamma* which casts doubt on cherished conceptions of Buddhahood. With regard to this, J. S. Walters points to the four-fold classification of *kamma* reported by Buddhaghosa in chapter 19 of his *Visuddhimagga*: 1) *kamma* the fruit of which will be experienced in this life; 2) *kamma* the fruit of which will be experienced in the next life; 3) *kamma* the fruit of which will be experienced in some future life; and 4) *kamma* the fruit of which will not be experienced at all (*ahosikamma*, literally "was-*kamma*"). The Buddha's sufferings were the results of long distant acts (*kamma* of the third type). According to J. S. Walters' interpretation, actions that resulted from the effects of these acts were themselves *ahosikamma* (*kamma* of the fourth type), and resulted in no further *kamma*. J. S. Walters notes that while there is no indication that this classification was formulated so as to answer the problem of the Buddha's bad *kamma*, the classification allows for an affirmation of *Pkp* which also rebuts the objections tradition had raised to it.

The Pāli canon as it now stands allows both natural causes and karmic causes for the misfortune in the Buddha's life. That the two types of explanation can be compatible each with the other has been touched on earlier. One need not preclude the other.

The *Pubbakammapiloti* (*Pkp*)

Pkp is found quoted in the *Paramattha-Dīpanī Udānaṭṭhakathā* of Dhammapālācariya. The edited text, which contains minor differences in readings from the edited text as given by *Ap*, can be found in *Ud-a.*[61] It is also repeated section-of-verse by section-of-verse with a lengthy commentary in Pāli in the *Visuddhajanavilāsinī nāma Apadānaṭṭhakathā.*[62] The edited text in *Ap*[63] and a translation of this text follow. A few significant variant readings are given as well in parentheses. Also given in parentheses are occasional readings from the Sinhalese edition of the *Apadāna* by the Venerable Pandita Talalle Dhammananda Thera when these clarify the text or are significant.[64] The edited text contains twelve *kammas*.

1. *Anotattasarâsanne ramaṇīye silātale*
   nānāratanapajjote nānāgandhavanantare
2. *Mahatā bhikkhusaṅghena pareto lokanāyako*
   āsīno vyākari tattha pubbakammāni attano:
3. *'Suṇotha bhikkhavo mayham yaṃ kammaṃ pakatam mayā*
   pilotiyassa kammassa buddhatthe (*Ap S: buddhatte*) *pi vipaccati.*
4. *Munāli* (*v.l. Puḷāni*) *nām' ahaṃ dhutto pubbe aññāsu jātisu*
   paccekabuddhaṃ Surabhim abbhācikkhim adūsakaṃ.
5. *Tena kammavipākena niraye saṃsariṃ ciraṃ*
   bahū vassasahassāni dukkhaṃ vedesiṃ vedanaṃ.
6. *Tena kammâvasesena idha pacchimake bhave*
   abbhakkhānaṃ mayā laddhaṃ Sundarīkāya kāraṇā.

---

61. *Ud-a*, pp. 263-66.
62. For edited text of this, see *Ap-a*, pp. 114-27 and pp. 479-80.
63. *Ap*, pp. 299-301.
64. Venerable Pandita Talalle Dhammananda Thera, 1961-83 (hence, *Ap S*), Part I, pp. 548-53.

7. *Sabbābhibhussa Buddhassa Nando nām' āsi sāvako*
tam abbhakkhāya niraye ciraṃ saṃsaritam mayā.

8. *Dasavassasahassāni niraye saṃsariṃ ciraṃ*
manussabhāvaṃ laddhâham abbhakkhānaṃ bahuṃ labhiṃ.

9. *Tena kammâvasesena Ciñca mānavikā mamaṃ*
abbhakkhāsi abhūtena janakāyassa aggato.

10. *Brāhmaṇo sutavā āsim ahaṃ sakkatapūjito*
mahāvane pañcasate mante vācemi māṇave.

11. *Tatthâgato Isigaṇo* (see *v.l.*; *Ap S*: *isi Bhīmo*)
pañcâbhiññāmahiddhiko (*v.l.*, *Ap S*: *pañcâbhiñño mahiddhiko*)
tañ câham āgataṃ disvā abbhācikkhim adūsakaṃ.

12. *Tato 'ham avacaṃ sisse: kāmabhogī ayaṃ isi*
mayhaṃ vibhāsamānassa (*Ap S*: *pi bhāsamānassa*)
anumodiṃsu māṇavā.

13. *Tato māṇavakā sabbe bhikkhamānā kulākule* (*v.l.*, *Ap S*: *kule kule*)
mahājanassa ahaṃsu (*Ap S*: *āhaṃsu*)*: kāmabhogī ayaṃ isi.*

14. *Tena kammavipākena pañcabhikkhusatā ime*
abbhakkhānaṃ labhuṃ sabbe Sundarīkāya kāraṇā.

15. *Dvemātā-bhātaro pubbe dhanahetu haniṃ ahaṃ*
pakkhipiṃ giriduggesu silāya ca apiṃsayiṃ.

16. *Tena kammavipākena Devadatto silaṃ khipi*
aṅguṭṭham piṃsayī pāde mama pāsānasakkharā.

17. *Pure 'haṃ dārako hutvā kīḷamāno mahāpathe*
paccekabuddhaṃ disvāna magge sakalikaṃ dahiṃ.

18. *Tena kammavipākena idha pacchimake bhave*
vadhatthaṃ maṃ Devadatto abhimāre payojayi.

19. *Hatthâroho pure āsiṃ paccekamunim uttamaṃ*
piṇḍāya vicarantaṃ tam āsādesiṃ gajen' ahaṃ.

20. *Tena kammavipākena bhanto Nāḷāgirī gajo*
Giribbaje puravare dāruṇo mam upāgamī.

21. *Rājâhaṃ patthivo (v.l. pattiko, satthako) āsiṃ sattiyā purisaṃ haniṃ*
tena kammavipākena niraye paccasiṃ bhusaṃ.

22. *Kammuṇo (v.l., Ap S: Kammuno) tassa sesena c'ādiṇṇam (Ap S: idani) sakalaṃ mama*
pāde chaviṃ pakopesi na hi kammaṃ panassati (v.l., Ap S: vinassati).

23. *Ahaṃ kevaṭṭagāmasmim ahuṃ kevaṭṭadārako*
macchake ghātite disvā janayiṃ somanassakaṃ.

24. *Tena kammavipākena sīsadukkham ahu mama*
Sakkesu haññamānesu yadā hani Viḍuḍabho.

25. *Phussassâhaṃ pāvacane sāvake paribhāsayiṃ*
yavaṃ khādatha bhuñjatha mā ca bhuñjatha sāliyo.

26. *Tena kammavipākena temāsaṃ khāditaṃ yavaṃ*
nimantito brāhmaṇena verajjāyaṃ vasiṃ tadā.

27. *Nibbuddhe vattamānamhi Mallaputtaṃ nisedhayiṃ (Ap S: niheṭhayiṃ)*
tena kammavipākena piṭṭhidukkham ahu mama.

28. *Tikicchako aham āsiṃ seṭṭhiputtaṃ virecayiṃ*
tena kammavipākena hoti pakkhandikā mama.

29. *Avacâhaṃ Jotipālo sugataṃ Kassapaṃ tadā:*
kuto nu bodhi muṇḍassa bodhi paramadullabhā?

30. *Tena kammavipākena ācariṃ dukkaraṃ bahuṃ*
chabbassān' Uruvelāyaṃ tato bodhim apāpuṇiṃ.

31. *Nâhaṃ etena maggena pāpuṇiṃ bodhim uttamaṃ*
kummaggena gavesissaṃ pubbakammena kārito (Ap S: vārito).

32. *Puññapāpaparikhīṇo sabbasantāpavajjito*
asoko anupāyāso nibbāyissam anāsavo.'

33. *Evaṃ jino viyākāsi bhikkhusaṅghassa aggato*
sabbâbhiññābalappatto Anotatte mahāsare ti.
Itthaṃ sudaṃ bhagavā attano pubbacaritaṃ Pubbakammapiloti nāma Buddhâpadānaṃ dhamma-pariyāyam abhāsi.
Pubbakammapiloti nāma Buddhâpadānaṃ samattaṃ.

1–2. Near beautiful Anotatta Lake on a slab of rock having the lustre of diverse gems, there within a forest with all kinds of scents, the Lord of the World seated with a great assembly of monks explained his deeds done in previous existences:

3. "Listen, monks, to my deed that I have done. Even for one having Buddha(hood) as his attainment (*Ap S*: Even in Buddhahood) there are results (or, fruit) from a small rag of a deed (or, from the thread of a deed).

4–6. "In a past life, among other lives, I was a scoundrel named Munāli. I slandered the innocent *paccekabuddha* Surabhi. As a consequence of that deed, I transmigrated in hell for a long time. Many thousands of rainy seasons I experienced painful feelings. By the remainder of that deed, in this last life I received slander because of Sundarīkā.

7–9. "There was a disciple named Nanda of the Buddha Sabbābhibhū. Having slandered him, I transmigrated in hell a long time. For a long time, I transmigrated thousands of decades in hell. After I obtained human existence, I received much slander. By the remainder of that deed, the Brahman girl Ciñca slandered me falsely in front of a group of people.

10–14. "I was a Brahman learned in religious knowledge, honored and revered. In a great forest, I was teaching 500 Brahman youths the Vedas. Isigaṇa (*Ap S*: The holy man Bhīma; see *v.l.*) possessing the five higher knowledges of great power arrived there. And having seen him come, I slandered him (even though he was) innocent. Further, I said to the pupils: 'This holy man is enjoying sensual pleasures.' The Brahman youths were thankful of my illumination (*Ap S*: of my saying so). Afterward, all the Brahman youths, begging alms from household to household, said to the people: 'This holy man is enjoying sensual pleasures.' As a consequence of that deed, these 500 monks all received slander because of Sundarīkā.

15–16. "Previously, there were the brothers of two mothers. I killed for the sake of wealth. I hurled (my brother) onto a difficult mountain road and I pounded (him) with a stone. As a consequence of that deed, Devadatta cast a rock. A fragment of rock pounded the great toe on my foot.

17–18. "Before, being a child, while playing on a high road (and) seeing a *paccekabuddha*, I put a little piece of rock (or, a potsherd) on the road. As a consequence of that deed, in this last life Devadatta, having killing me as his goal, took into service bandits.

19–20. "Before, I was an elephant driver. I assailed with an elephant the highest *paccekamuni* wandering about for alms. As a consequence of that deed, the elephant Nāḷāgiri, swaggering and pitiless, came at me in the noble city of Rājagaha.

21–22. "I was an earthly king.[65] I killed a man with a dagger. As a consequence of that deed, I was boiled in hell vehemently. By the remainder of that deed, it hurt the skin on my foot, which was entirely split open (*Ap S*: now it hurt all the skin on my foot). A deed does not cease to be (*v.l.*, *Ap S*: does not perish).

23–24. "I was a child of a fisherman in a hamlet of fishermen. Having seen fish killed, I was happy. As a consequence of that deed I had a (bad) headache when Viḍuḍabha struck at the Sākyans, killing (them).

25–26. "I reviled disciples of the word of Phussa (saying): 'Eat and munch (rough) barley, but do not eat (soft) rice!' As a consequence of that deed, barley was munched for three months. Invited by a Brahman, I lived in Verajjā then.

27. "While wrestling was taking place, I restrained (*Ap S*: injured) the son of a wrestler. As a consequence of that deed, I had backache(s).

28. "I was a physician. I purged the son of a wealthy merchant. As a consequence of that deed, I had diarrhea (or, dysentery).

29–30. "I was Jotipāla, and I said at that time to the *sugata* Kassapa: 'How is the enlightenment of a baldheaded ascetic the enlightenment that is highest and hard to obtain?' As a consequence of that deed, I practiced much austerity for six years in Uruvelā. Thereupon (only), I attained enlightenment.

---

65. For 'earthly', *v.l.* footsoldier, or caravan merchant. But how to construe? Perhaps we should understand, a king going on foot, or a king belonging to a caravan.

31–32. "I did not attain the highest enlightenment by this path. Done (?) by a previous deed (*Ap S*: Obstructed by a previous deed), I strove by the wrong path. (Both) merit and sin extinct, excluded from all torments, free from sorrow, serene, free from the four intoxicants,[66] I was extinguished."

33. The Victor, grown strong with all higher knowledge (*abhiñña*), illuminated just so in front of the assemblage of monks at the great lake Anotatta. Thus the Lord spoke his previous behaviour, a disquisition on the law, the *Apadāna* of the Buddha named "The Small Rag (*i.e.* Remnant; or perhaps, Thread) of Previous Deeds". The *Apadāna* of the Buddha named "The Small Rag (or, Thread) of Previous Deeds" is brought to an end.

66. Sensuality, rebirth (lust of life), speculation, and ignorance.

The *Pubbakammapiloti* as in the *Detiskarma padārthayi*

UP adds three verses in Pāli to the above edited *Apadāna* text.

Toward the beginning of the text it adds an additional *kamma*, an action and its consequence, in two verses. It can be suggested that this is original since the first *kamma* of *Ap* reads, *pubbe aññāsu jātisu*, "in a past life, among other lives", the implication being that the narration is a continuation. These two verses as in *UP* are:

> *Gopāliko pure āsīt (=Skt. 3 s. impf.) gāvit pāvemi gocaraṃ /*
> *pivante viludakaṃ gāviṃ disvāṇa yaṃ nadīṃ //*
> *tena kammavipākena idha pañcemake gavē /*
> *uddakatāya ghate mayhaṃ susitaya mahānadiṃ //*

Corrected, the text would probably read:

> *Gopālako pure āsiṃ gāviṃ pājemi gocaraṃ /*
> *pivantim vil(?)udakaṃ gāviṃ disvāna yaṃ nādaṃ (na adaṃ > nadaṃ > nādaṃ) //*
> *tena kammavipākena idha pacchimake bhave /*
> *udakatthāya (udaka-atthāya) ghaṭe mayhaṃ sussitāyaṃ (sussitā ayaṃ) mahānadī //*

> "Previously I was a cowherd. I drove a cow to pasture.
> Seeing the cow drink muddy water, I did not allow it.
> As a consequence of that deed, now in this last life
> For the sake of water in my bowl, this great river was (entirely) dried up."

The metre here is defective in the third *pāda* of each of the two verses.

The third additional verse, at the end of the Pāli listing of *kammas*, before the additional *kammas* in Sinhalese alone, after being corrected on the basis of parallel text, reads:

> *susukhaṃ vata jīvāma yesaṃ no natthi kiñcanaṃ /*
> *pītibhakkhā bhavissāma devā ābhassarā yathā //*
>
> "We live happily, those who are tranquil, even though there is nothing with us. We will thrive on happiness, just as the radiant gods."

This verse as in *UP* is much corrupted, though its general outlines are clear enough that it can be identified. The verse occurs in the *Piṇḍa Sutta* of the *Saṃyutta Nikāya*. In this *sutta* due to a plot of Māra the Buddha was compelled to starve, as he did not obtain anything when he went in quest of alms. Seeing the Buddha with an empty bowl Māra jokingly remarked that the Buddha was evidently afflicted with hunger. Thereupon the Buddha recited this verse.[67] The verse also appears in the *Mahājanaka Jātaka*,[68] and in the *Sukhavagga* of the *Dhammapada*.[69] The explanation for the occurrence of this verse here comes in *BN*. It is the incident of the *Piṇḍa Sutta* that is related in this place in that manuscript. The Sinhalese text is missing here, though, in *UP*. And the text of the following story in *UP* is so corrupt that except for a few key words it cannot be read.

In *BN* only the first two verses noted here are indicated. The third verse is indicated in part in Sinhalese in the Sinhalese retelling of the *Piṇḍa Sutta*. Before the first two verses, however, its word-for-word rendition indicates incompletely still another added verse. The three of *these* verses as in *BN* are found with variations in a footnote in *Ap S*.[70] The extra verse of *BN* is found

---

67. See the text as in *S*, vol. 1, pp. 113–14, and the translation of *KS*, vol. 1, pp. 143–44.

68. *J*, vol. 6, p. 55 (*Jātaka* no. 539, vs. 128/248) and *SBFB*, vol. 6, p. 32.

69. See *Dh*, p. 30, vs. 200; J. R. Carter and M. Palihawadana, 1987, p. 255; Irving Babbitt, 1936, p. 32; Nārada Thera, 1954, p. 56; F. Max Müller, 2000, p. 24.

70. *Ap S*, Part I, p. 548.

embedded in the third verse of the edited text as in *Ap*. It is noted in the Sinhalese edition that these three verses are found in Thai manuscripts. These verses are:

> *suṇātha bhikkhave mayhaṃ kammaṃ pakataṃ mayā,*
> *ekam araññikaṃ bhikkhuṃ disvā dinnaṃ pilotikaṃ.*
> *patthitaṃ paṭhamaṃ buddhaṃ buddhattāya mayā tadā,*
> *pilotikassa kammassa buddhattepi vipaccati[.]*
> *Gopālako pure āsiṃ gāviṃ pājeti gocaraṃ,*
> *pivantiṃ udakaṃ āvilaṃ gāviṃ disvā nivārayiṃ.*
> *tena kammavipākena idha pacchimake bhave,*
> *pipāsito yadicchakaṃ na hi pātuṃ labhāmahaṃ.*

> "Listen, monks, to my deed that I have done. Having seen a certain forest monk, I gave a little piece of cloth. First I wished at that time for the perfect enlightenment of a Buddha. Even in Buddhahood, there are results (or, fruit) from the small rag of a deed (or, from the thread of a deed). Previously, I was a cowherd. He drove a cow to pasture. Seeing the cow drink muddy water, I did not allow it. As a consequence of that deed, now in this last life When thirsty, I certainly do not get (water) to drink according to liking."

BN, for the *UP* reading, *viludakaṃ*, reads *āvidakaṃ*, indicating that this should go back to the reading as in the Sinhalese printed text, *udakaṃ āvilaṃ*, except perhaps with the two words transposed. The metre with this reading, however, is also defective.

The Thai edition in *Mahidol U CD-ROM* contains these verses with occasional variation as part of its text of the *Apadāna*. In the Burmese edition in *CS CD-ROM* this extra text is repeated in a footnote with only occasional variation in the last line. This text is:

> *Suṇātha bhikkhave mayhaṃ yaṃ kammaṃ pakataṃ mayā*
> *ekaṃ araññikaṃ bhikkhuṃ disvā dinnaṃ pilotikaṃ.*
> *Patthitaṃ paṭhamaṃ buddhaṃ buddhatāya mayā tadā*
> *pilotiyassa kammassa budhatepi vipaccati[.]*

Gopālako pure āsiṃ gāviṃ pājeti gocaraṃ
pivantiṃ udakaṃ āvilaṃ gāviṃ disvā nivārayiṃ.
Tena kammavipākena idha pacchimake bhave pipāsito (*CS CD-ROM: vipāsito*) *yathicchakaṃ* (*CS CD-ROM: yadicchakaṃ*) *na hi pātuṃ labhāmahaṃ.*

The translation would read the same as that given for the Sinhalese edition text above.

In *UP* and *BN* we have these extra verses as given in Thai manuscripts indicated in a Sinhalese text, though with the last line different in *UP*.

BN also begins with a Pāli verse that I have not been able to locate elsewhere in the canon. This verse reads:

Bodhisatto atītasmiṃ pūretvā dasapāramī
pāpakaṃ dhammaṃ kārento saṃsāre saṃsaran ṭhito.

"Before fulfilling the ten perfections, the Bodhisatta abided transmigrating in the ocean of rebirth performing sinful practice."

In the later Pāli literature there is mentioned a group of ten perfections (*dasa pāramiyo*) as the perfect exercise of the ten principal virtues of a Bodhisatta.[71] It is very possible that this verse is original to our Pāli text but dropped out, as did the

---

71. These are *dāna* (perfection in giving, or liberality), *sīla* (perfection in morality), *nekkhamma* (renunciation), *paññā* (wisdom), *viriya* (energy), *khanti* (patience), *sacca* (truthfulness), *adhiṭṭhāna* (resolution), *mettā* (loving kindness), and *upekkhā* (equanimity). See *PED*, p. 454b and Nyanatiloka, [1952], pp. 125–26. In the Mahāyāna scriptures, where the *pāramitās* occupy a much more prominent place, a partly differing list of six is given: liberality, morality, patience, energy, concentration (or meditation), and wisdom. Later this list was expanded to ten by the addition of skill in means necessary to help others, profound resolution to produce enlightenment, the ten powers (*bala*), and practice of the *jhānas* (progression through various mental states culminating in enhanced psychic vitality). Rarely the list enumerates five or seven *pāramitās*. See T. Skorupski, 2002. Alternately see É. Lamotte, 1949. And see T. O. Ling, 1972, pp. 205–206; and further *BHSGD*, vol. 2, pp. 341b–342a.

other verses that are found in the Thai Pāli canon. S. M. Cutler mentions that although the *Pkp* is described as a *buddhāpadāna*, its connection with the Buddha and with the *Buddhāpadāna*, the first section of the *Apadāna* collection, is obscured by its placement as *Therāpadāna* 390 (no. 387 in *Ap*). She then adds that it is possible that the *Pkp* was originally linked in some way with the *Buddhāpadāna*.[72] She further points out that in the *Apadāna* collection, the *pāramitās* are the subject of four verses, verses 73–76, of the *Buddhāpadāna*.[73] Is it possible that we have here a remnant of the original linkage?

Other variant readings for *Pkp* in *UP* include noticeably the omission of verse 11 in the edited text above which mentions specifically Isigaṇa, or perhaps a holy man Bhīma. Also, for *Suṇotha bhikkhavo* in verse 3a, *UP* reads *Suṇetha bhikkhave*. For *vipaccati* in verse 3d, it reads *vividhati*. For *jātisu* in verse 4b, *jātiyā*. For *manussabhāvaṃ* in verse 8c, *manusayoniṃ*. For *aham āsiṃ* in verse 28a, *pure āsiṃ*. For *virecayiṃ* in verse 28b, *virocayiṃ*. For *pubbakammena* in verse 31d, *puṅkakammena*. The latter as a reading is probably derived from an abbreviation for *pubbakammena* in the Sinhalese script. It is repeated again in the final summation of the Sinhalese text.

72. S. M. Cutler, 1994, p. 14.
73. S. M. Cutler, 1994, p. 16.

The *Destiskarma padārthkayi* (*BN* and *UP*)

A problem occurs as to why our text refers to itself as treating thirty-two *kammas*, since in *UP* there are only seventeen *kammas* treated, and in *BN* there are only twenty-two *kammas* treated. The Pāli text as in *Ap*, as noted, contains only twelve *kammas*. For a while I considered counting actions and their consequences separately for *UP*. If we do this and count two two-fold consequences separately as two *kammas* each, we arrive at the number thirty-two. This falls apart, though, when we turn to *BN*, and when we consider that after each action and its consequence(s) in the Sinhalese text, there is the refrain, "This, O monks, is one *karma*."

The more likely solution is that the number thirty-two in the title of the text is symbolic, and that it is specified perhaps to indicate that the *kammas* in the text are representative of the totality of the Buddha's bad *kamma*. Note that the number of Vedic deities is calculated to be thirty-two. These represent the entirety of the *sat*, the realm of being. Also, there are thirty-two characteristic marks of a *mahāpurisa*, a great man, thirty-two impurities of the body, etc. Also note that *Ap* contains thirty-two verses before the final summation. This suggests that the extra verses found in Thai manuscripts, with an extra *kamma*, were dropped to achieve a text of thirty-two verses total. As noted above, there is indication in the current edited text that these verses are original. So also, perhaps, the extra Pāli verse found at the beginning of *BN*. In general, there is auspicious value given to the number thirty-two in Indic tradition. This may be behind the explanation as to why the Sinhalese tradition has expanded the number of *kammas* to thirty-two, and why the *Apadāna* tradition has manipulated the number of verses in *Pkp*.

There follow the stories as told in *BN*. These are fuller than the Pāli text. I provide here the account as in *BN* since its text is less corrupt that that of *UP*, and since it contains in all but one case not only the additional stories of *UP* but others as well. The additional story of *UP* not found in *BN* is given at the end of the presentation of *BN* along with a section of prose summation found in *UP* but not in *BN*. The latter corresponds to *Pkp*, vss. 31–32, and 33. Along with each story as given in *BN* there are given identifications of persons and places mentioned, cross-references to *DPPN*, and some additional notes. Also noted are any significant differences in the stories as they are related in *UP*.

Buddha confessed at Anavatatta (P. Anotatta) Lake[74] that when he was a Bodhisatta he did *akusalakarmas* (unwholesome deeds) and experienced the consequences.[75]

Ia. "I was born as a householder in a family of herdsmen. I was driving herd to pasture. I prevented cattle from drinking muddy water in a pool.[76] This was a demeritorious deed.

---

74. Anotatta Lake is one of the seven great lakes of Himavā. Five mountain peaks, Sudassanakūṭa, Citrakūṭa, Kāḷakūṭa, Gandhamādana, and Kelāsa surround it. A wind called Siñcanakavāta (sprinkling wind) takes water from the Anotatta Lake and sprinkles the Gandhamādana Mountain with it. To be bathed in the waters of the lake is to be thoroughly cleansed. The Buddha would often go to Anotatta for his ablutions and proceed from there to Uttarakuru for alms, returning to the lake to have a meal and spend the hot part of the day on its banks. Sometimes the Buddha would go there with a company of monks and preach or make proclamations. For Anotatta Lake see *DPPN*, vol. 1, pp. 96–99.

75. An explanation in *BN* states that this took place on Gandhamādana Mountain. Gandhamādana is one of the five mountain ranges that encircle Anotatta. It is beyond the seven ranges of Cullakāḷa, Mahākāḷa, Nāgapaliveṭhana, Candagabbha, Suriyagabbha, Suvaṇṇapassa, and Himavā. It is crowned with a tableland, is green in color, and is covered with medicinal plants. It is not explicitly mentioned that all *pacceka-buddhas* die on Gandhamādana, but the inference seems to be such. See *DPPN*, vol. 1, pp. 746–48.

76. That the Sinhalese text here relates the story entirely in the first person reflects the Pāli text as in *UP* as against the Pāli text for this story reported elsewhere (see above).

Ib. "As a result, in this birth as Buddha, when the great *thera* (elder) Ānanda[77] went to a river with clear water to fetch me water to quench my thirst, the water in that river dried up. This, O monks, is one *karma*.[78]

IIa. "I was born in a family (P. and Sinh. *kula*) of tailors named Munāli.[79] I observed *paccekabuddhas*. I came across a virtuous *paccekabuddha* walking in the city begging for alms. With a defiled mind I abused him, accusing him of saying and doing things which he had not said or done. I said that ascetic had been having sexual intercourse with

77. Ānanda was one of the principal disciples of the Buddha. He was a cousin of the Buddha and was deeply attached to him. During the first twenty years after the enlightenment, the Buddha did not have the same personal servants all the time. From time to time various monks looked after him. At the end of twenty years, at an assembly of the monks, the Buddha declared that he was advanced in years and desired to have somebody as his personal body-servant, one who would respect his wishes in every way. All the great disciples offered their services, but were rejected by the Buddha. Ānanda alone was left. The Buddha signified that he wished to have Ānanda, and the latter agreed to accept the post on certain conditions which insured that people would not say that he was performing his services for special considerations, and which insured that people would trust him and realize that the Buddha had real regard for him. After this, for twenty-five years Ānanda waited on the Buddha, following him like a shadow, bringing him water and toothpick, washing his feet, accompanying him everywhere, sweeping his cell, and so forth. See *DPPN*, vol. 1, pp. 249–68. The above story in *BN* and *UP* is not mentioned in *DPPN*.

78. This story reflects the Pāli verse as in *UP*. The Sinhalese story as in *UP*, further reflecting the second additional verse added to the Pāli text as in *UP*, translates, "Now in this life, when thirsty, I asked Ānanda to bring some water. He went to the river with my bowl. The river usually had clear, cool water. When Ānanda went, it dried *UP*. This is one of the consequences of my past actions."

79. Citing the *Apadāna* account, Munāli is mentioned briefly in *DPPN*, vol. 2, p. 645. According to the Sinhalese account above, Munāli is the name of a tailor family. The Thai edition of the *Apadāna* in *Mahidol U CD-ROM* gives the name as Punāli. See the *v.l.* in the text above, Puḷāni. The Burmese edition in *CS CD-ROM* gives the name as Munāḷi.

women. Because of this past action, I was scorched in hell (P. and Sinh. *niraya*) for a long time.

IIb. "In this last life, as a consequence of this, I had a similar accusation about an ascetic woman named Sundarī (P. Sundarī, Sundarīkā). She has been telling the public that she has been living with me in the perfumed chamber. In this way, she has disgraced me.[80] This, O monks, is one *karma*.

IIIa. "During the time of the Buddha named Vessabhū,[81] I abused unwarrantably one of his disciples named Nanda[82] saying that a certain woman had become pregnant by him. I thereby insulted him. Because of that I have been boiled and wandering in hell for a long time. This is due to the accusation of a virtuous monk. Because of accusations of this type, I have been undergoing torment for thousands and thousands of years in hell. Then when I was born as a human I have been abused and insulted in various places of things that I neither said nor did.[83]

IIIb. "In my last birth as Buddha, when I was preaching to the fourfold assembly at Jetavana Grove,[84] a courtesan Ciñcī (P.

---

80. For a fuller version of the incident involving Sundarī, see *DPPN*, vol. 2, pp. 1216–17.

81. Vessabhū was the twenty-first of the twenty-four Buddhas. He is mentioned as having been sixty cubits in height, and to have lived for 60,000 years. See *DPPN*, vol. 2, pp. 947–48. *Pkp* refers to him as Sabbābhibhū.

82. Nanda was a disciple of the Buddha Sabbābhibhū according to the Pāli text. It was as a result of slandering him in a previous life that the Buddha in his last life was slandered by Ciñca-mānavikā. See *DPPN*, vol. 2, p. 13. *DPPN* construes this event also to have taken place during the Buddha's former life as Munāli. *UP* omits the name of the disciple accused by the Buddha in his former life in its Sinhalese text.

83. For this story, given more fully, in Buddhist Sanskrit Hīnayāna tradition see J. J. Jones, 1949–56, vol. 1, pp. 29–39.

84. Jetavana is a park in Sāvatthi, in which was built the Anāthapiṇḍikārāma. When the Buddha accepted Anāthapiṇḍika's invitation to visit Sāvatthi the latter, seeking a suitable place for the Buddha's residence, discovered this park belonging to Jetakumāra. When he asked to be allowed to buy it, Jeta's reply was: "Not even if you could cover the whole place with money." Anāthapiṇḍika said he would

Ciñcī, Ciñca-mānavikā) of that city reviled me feigning that she was with child because of me.[85] Ciñcī had a bunch of sticks tied to her stomach and covered it with a cloth, and when I was preaching a discourse, she came in front of me and insulted me in this manner: 'Now you are preaching to *siṭṭhāna* (P. *seṭṭhi*, banker) Anepiṇḍu (P. Anāthapiṇḍika)[86] and Visākhā,[87] but I am

---

buy it at that price. And when Jeta answered that he had no intention of making a bargain, the matter was taken before the Lords of Justice. They decided that if the price mentioned were paid, Anāthapiṇḍika had the right of purchase. Anāthapiṇḍika had gold brought down in carts and covered Jetavana with pieces laid side by side. Anāthapiṇḍika built on the grounds dwelling rooms, retiring rooms, store rooms and service halls, halls with fireplaces, closets, cloisters, halls for exercise, wells, bathrooms, ponds, open and roofed sheds, etc. The Buddha spent nineteen rainy seasons in Jetavana. It is said that after the Migāramātupāsāda came into being, the Buddha would dwell alternately in Jetavana and Migāramātupāsāda, often spending the day in one and the night in the other. Near Jetavana was evidently a monastery of heretics where Ciñcī spent her nights while hatching her conspiracy against the Buddha. See *DPPN*, vol. 1, pp. 963–66.

85. For Ciñcī and her conspiracy against the Buddha, see *DPPN*, vol. 1, p. 864 under Ciñca-mānavakā. Ciñcī is standardly said to have come before the Buddha and charged him with irresponsibility and callousness in that he made no provisions for her pregnancy as he preached to a vast congregation. The references to Ciñcī in *DPPN* simply refer to Ciñcī as the member of a heretical ascetic order that found their gains had grown less owing to the popularity of the Buddha. According to the Sinhalese account in *UP*, though, they are Niganthas, or Jains. This is not reflected in *BN*.

86. Anāthapiṇḍika was a banker of Sāvatthi who became famous because of his unparalleled generosity to the Buddha. See *DPPN*, vol. 1, pp. 67–72.

87. Visākhā was related to Anāthapiṇḍika by marriage. His daughter-in-law was Visākhā's youngest sister. See *DPPN*, vol. 1, p. 68 and vol. 2, p. 904. Visākhā was the chief among the female lay disciples of the Buddha, declared by him to be the foremost of those who ministered to the order. Visākhā owned such a great reputation for bringing good fortune that the people of Sāvatthi always invited her to their houses on festivals and holidays. Visākhā fed 500 monks daily at her house.

left without requisites for my maternity. Now I am in advanced pregnancy and you are trying to entrust me to these people in the assembly without supplying me with oil and pepper.' She insulted me in this manner. Then (a god) came as a rat and cut the band around her body. The people in the assembly took stones and clubs and beat (perhaps, killed) her.[88] This, O monks, is one *karma*.

IVa. "Once I was a Brahman well-versed in the three Vedas. For the sake of gain, I wanted to teach the three Vedas to 500 Brahmans. They were learning the three Vedas and were rewarding me. At that time an ascetic who had attained to the fivefold knowledge and eightfold attainments came to that forest. Thinking that if the students were to come to know the greatness of the ascetic they would not treat me well, I told these: 'This ascetic is associating with a woman. He is devoid of virtue, and is crafty. Believe me.' So I insulted this sage who possessed psychic powers. When this ascetic went in search of alms to the village, the 500 students went to the people of the village and told them that this ascetic was attached to the fivefold sensual desires, was a thief, and was cunning. So the students got the citizens to insult the ascetic.

IVb. "Because of this bad deed, in this last birth of mine when I was travelling in the city of Kosambī[89] begging alms, a Brahman lady named Māgandi (P. Māgandiyā) conceived hatred toward me, bribed the citizens of Kosambī, and told them: 'When Gautama comes to this city, you should insult him. You should chase this wretched fellow out of the city.' At the time ... (the Blessed One) went to the city, Māgandi collected some people from the city and began to scold me. She abused the Buddha and

---

In the afternoon she visited the Buddha, and, after listening to his sermon, would go round the monastery inquiring into the needs of the monks and nuns. See *DPPN*, vol. 2, pp. 900–904.

88. In the corresponding Buddhist Sanskrit Hīnayāna story in the *Mahāvastu*, the name of the Buddha's accuser in this life is lost. See J. J. Jones, 1949–56, vol. 1, p. 38.

89. Kosambī was the capital of the Vatsas or Vaṃsas. See *DPPN*, vol. 1, pp. 692–94.

the *saṅgha* in this manner: 'Ye cunning recluse! Idiot! ... Confused one! One like a camel! Bull! ... You like one born in hell! You are like a four-footed animal! You are not destined to attain *nirvāṇa* (P. *nibbāna*)! You will always be in misery!' They chased me for a full six days in this manner.[90] This, O monks, is one *karma*.

Va. "There were two brothers of two mothers (and one father). The elder brother killed the younger brother by piercing him and throwing him off a precipice to get his property, etc. I was this brother. Because of that evil deed I was born in hell for a number of years.

Vb. "Because of that demeritorious deed, in this present life when I was walking on the Gijikulu Mountain (P. Gijjhakūṭapabbata)[91] Devadatta rolled on me rocks from that

---

90. Māgandiyā had been offered in marriage to the Buddha by her father, but the offer was rejected, the Buddha referring to her as a "vessel of filth". Her uncle took her to Udena, king of Kosambī, who made her his chief consort. When the Buddha came to Kosambī, Māgandiyā planned her revenge. Among other plans, Māgandiyā hired a slave to revile and abuse the Buddha in the streets. Ānanda suggested to the Buddha that they should go elsewhere. The Buddha answered: "I am like the elephant who has entered the fray. I must endure the darts that come upon me." After seven days the abuse ceased. See *DPPN*, vol. 2, pp. 596–97. *BN* refers to the abuse as having lasted a full six days. *UP*, though, reads here that the abuse lasted seven days. The story as related by *DPPN* is related differently in the Sinhalese account above. Also, *Pkp* does not mention the incident. It refers instead to the 500 monks, who were Brahmans who reviled a holy man named Isigaṇa, or a holy man named Bhīma perhaps, at the Buddha's instigation in a previous life, as having been slandered by Sundarīkā in this life. The Sinhalese text, though not mentioning by name Isigaṇa, or a holy man Bhīma, relates the earlier deed to the behavior of Māgandiyā toward the Buddha. It thus relates the earlier deed to a *kamma* of the Buddha himself. Isigaṇa and Bhīma are mentioned briefly, with this passage as the reference, in *DPPN*, vol. 1, p. 319 and vol. 2, p. 382.

91. Gijjhakūṭa is one of the five hills encircling Rājagaha. The Buddha seems to have been attracted to its solitude, and is mentioned as having visited it on several occasions, sometimes even in the dark, in drizzling rain, while Māra made unsuccessful attempts to frighten him. See *DPPN*, vol. 1, pp. 762–64.

mountain, whereupon two rocks sprang from the earth and held them. But a particle of one came and struck my foot like a strong man attacking with an axe.[92] This, O monks, is one *karma.*

VIa. "Once as a child I was playing on a road with other children. I, having seen a *paccekabuddha* passing that way for begging in the city, obstructed his way with stones and gravel. Then I threw a stone at him.[93]

VIb. "As a consequence of this bad action, when I was living in Nigrodhārāma[94] in this last birth my father-in-law, the Sākyan king Suprabuddha (P. Suppabuddha), developed a great hatred against me saying that I left his daughter Yasodharā[95]

---

92. Devadatta was the son of the maternal uncle of the Buddha, Suppabuddha, and the brother of the Buddha's wife, Bhaddakaccānā, or Yasodharā. When the Buddha visited Kapilavatthu after the enlightenment and preached to the Sākyans, Devadatta was converted. For some time he seems to have enjoyed great honor in the Order. Devadatta was later suspected of evil wishes. About eight years before the Buddha's death, Devadatta, eager for gain and favor, and jealous of the Buddha's fame, attempted to win over Ajātasattu. The success of this encouraged Devadatta in his schemes, and he conceived the idea of taking the Buddha's place as leader of the *saṅgha.* Among other schemes, one day, when the Buddha was walking on the slopes of Gijjhakūṭa, Devadatta hurled down on the Buddha a great rock. Two peaks sprung *UP* from the ground, thereby arresting its rushing advance. But a splinter struck the Buddha's foot, causing blood to flow. According to *DPPN*, *Apadāna* ii.300 f. [= *Pkp*?] explains that all the plans of Devadatta to harm the Buddha were the result of the Buddha's previous evil deeds. See *DPPN*, vol. 1, pp. 1106–11 and vol. 1, p. 763.

93. For the little piece of rock, or perhaps potsherd of *Pkp*, the Sinhalese text as in *BN* substitutes stones and gravel. The Sinhalese text as in *UP* substitutes charcoal. *Pkp* does not note that a stone was thrown at the *paccekabuddha.*

94. Nigrodhārāma was a grove near Kapilavatthu where a residence was provided for the Buddha when he visited the city in the first year after his enlightenment. It belonged to a Sākyan named Nigrodha, who gave it to the Order. See *DPPN*, vol. 2, pp. 70–71.

95. Yasodharā is also known as Bhaddakaccā (or, Bhaddakaccānā) and Rāhulamātā, among other names. She was Gotama's wife and

and went begging in the street, and that I ordained his prince Devadatta without his consent. Then, when I was entering the inner city in the company of monks, he obstructed our way with a crowd of people … . I was therefore compelled to return to the monastery with my fellow monks.[96] Due to the evil deed of pelting stones at the *paccekabuddha*, Devadatta bribed 500 archers and made them shoot arrows at me when I was walking on Gijukulu Mountain. O monks, this is (still) another *karma*.[97]

Rāhula's mother. She was born the same day as the Bodhisatta, and married Gotama at the age of sixteen. Gotama left household life on the day of the birth of his son Rāhula. It is said that just before he left home he took a last look at his wife from the door of her room, not daring to go nearer lest he should awake her. When the Buddha paid his first visit to Kapilavatthu after the enlightenment, he begged in the street for alms on the second day of that visit. The news spread and Yasodharā looked out of her window to see if it were true. She saw the Buddha, and was struck by the glory of his personality. She then uttered eight verses in its praise. These verses have been handed down under the name of *Narasīhagāthā*. See *DPPN*, vol. 2, p. 693 and vol. 2, pp. 741–42 under Rāhulamātā.

96. Suppabuddha was a Sākyan prince, and the father of Bhaddakaccānā and Devadatta. Thus he was the father-in-law of the Buddha. It is said that he was offended by the Buddha deserting his daughter and for being hostile to Devadatta. One day he took strong drink and blocked the Buddha's path, refusing to move in spite of the repeated requests of the monks. The Buddha thereupon turned back. Ānanda seeing the Buddha smile and enquiring the reason for the smile, was told that at the end of seven days Suppabuddha would be swallowed *UP* by the earth at the foot of his stairs. Suppabuddha overheard this, and tried to prevent it from happening. But it came to pass as the Buddha had predicted. See *DPPN*, vol. 2, pp. 1220–21.

97. Neither *Pkp* nor *UP* mention the first part of the consequence noted in *BN* regarding Suppabuddha. *UP* reads only, "As a consequence of this bad action, now as Buddha in this past birth Devadatta has bribed 500 archers when I was walking about wandering the Gijjakūṭapabbata and they shot arrows at me. So monks, this is one of my *karmas*." *Pkp* refers to a bandit taken into service by Devadatta, who struck the Buddha. The Sinhalese text here refers to 500 archers bribed by Devadatta, who shot arrows at the Buddha. The story as related by *DPPN*, vol. 1, p. 1108 is

VIIa. "Once I was an elephant keeper. When I was riding an elephant, I met a *paccekabuddha* on my way and I turned the elephant toward him in order to frighten him for amusement.

VIIb. "As a consequence of that action, in this last birth of mine while I was going on my alms round in Rājagaha,[98] Devadatta set upon me (the elephant) Nālāgiri after giving it toddy to drink.[99] This, O monks, is one *karma*.

VIIIa. "Once I was in the service of a king.[100] On the order of the king, I stabbed a man. As a consequence of this action, I was boiled in hells for a long time. But even then the consequences of that action were not over.

VIIIb. "In this last birth as Buddha, the skin of my foot

---

that Devadatta instigated Ajātasattu to provide him with royal archers to shoot the Buddha. These were placed on different paths, one on one path, two on another, and so on *UP* to sixteen, and the plan was so laid that not one of them would survive to tell the tale. But when the Buddha approached the first man, he was terrified by the Buddha's majesty, and his body became stiff. The Buddha spoke kindly to him, and the man, throwing away his weapons, confessed his intended crime. The Buddha thereupon preached to him and, having converted him, sent him back by a different path. The other groups of archers, tired of waiting, gave *UP* the vigil and went away one after the other. The different groups were led to the Buddha by his *iddhi*-power, and he preached to them and converted them. The first man returned to Devadatta saying that he was unable to kill the Buddha because of his great *iddhi*-power.

98. Rājagaha was the capital of Magadha. It was one of the six chief cities of the Buddha's time. Rājagaha was closely associated with the Buddha's work. It is the scene of several important *suttas*. Many of the *vinaya* rules were enacted at Rājagaha. See *DPPN*, vol. 2, pp. 721–24.

99. By the story as told by *DPPN*, vol. 1, pp. 1108–1109, Devadatta persuaded elephant-keepers to let loose the fierce elephant Nālāgiri (or Dhanapāla), drunk with toddy, on a road by which the Buddha would pass. The news spread rapidly, and the Buddha was warned, but refused to turn back. As the elephant advanced he pervaded it with love, and thus completely subdued it. See also *DPPN*, vol. 2, p. 58.

100. According to *UP*, the Buddha in his former life was in the service of a king as a footsoldier. This latter is not specified in *BN*. *Pkp* would seem to read that the Buddha was in his former life an earthly king. But see note 65 above.

came off. This, O monks, is one *karma*.

IXa. "Once I was born as the son of a fisherman. I observed fishermen catching fish with their nets and putting the fish in a heap. I watched that heap of fish with joy. Because of that action, for several births I suffered from headaches.

IXb. "In this last birth as Buddha, I had headaches, too. As a result of this, my Sākyan relatives[101] of Kiṃbulvat (P. Kapilavatthu)[102] were killed and piled *UP* by Viḍūḍabha.[103] This, O monks, is one *karma*.

Xa. "Once I was a layman. At that time, a disciple monk of the Buddha Phussa[104] was learning Pāli texts. Seeing that the monk had abundant alms, I teased him saying: 'This monk's grains (barley) are good to eat. But of them, rice

101. For the Sākyas, see *DPPN*, vol. 2, pp. 969–72

102. Kapilavatthu was a city near the Himālaya. It was the capital of the Sākyans, to which tribe the Buddha belonged. Near the city was the Lumbinīvana where the Buddha was born. See *DPPN*, vol. 1, pp. 516–20.

103. Viḍūḍabha was the son of King Pasenadi of Kosala and the daughter of the Sākyan chieftain, Mahānāma, by a slave-girl, Nāgamuṇḍa. The Sākyans were vassals of King Pasenadi of Kosala. Pasenadi had wished to establish connection with the Buddha's family by marrying one of the daughters of a Sākyan chief. But the Sākyans decided that it would be beneath their dignity to marry one of their daughters to the king of Kosala. But as they dared not refuse Pasenadi's request, they solved the difficulty by giving him Mahānāma's daughter by a slave-girl. When Pasenadi discovered the trick, he deprived his wife and her son of all their honors, but restored them on the intervention of the Buddha. Later, when Viḍūḍabha, who had vowed vengeance on the Sākyans for the insult offered to his father, became king, he marched into Kapilavatthu and there massacred the Sākyans, including women and children. The Buddha felt himself powerless to save them from their fate because they had committed sin in a previous life by throwing poison into a river. Only a few escaped. See *DPPN*, vol. 2, pp. 971-72. The details of Viḍūḍabha's invasion of Kapilavatthu are given more fully in *DPPN*, vol. 1, pp. 517–18.

104. Phussa was the eighteenth of the twenty-four Buddhas. He lived for 90,000 years. His body was fifty-eight cubits high. See *DPPN*, vol. 2, p. 257.

made of *äl* paddy is good for me.'[105]

Xb. "As a result of the evil *karma* of asking a virtuous monk to eat barley grains out of abundant alms, now in my last birth as Buddha, when a Brahman invited me for alms during the *vas* season (P. *vassa*, rainy season retreat), Māra[106] made me (*i.e.*, him ?) forget that invitation. When I went to Verañjā, there was a famine there at the time and the 500 monks and myself came out of the village not obtaining any food.[107] Then we went to the market fair of 500 horse dealers who came from the province of Uttarāṅga.[108] Each horse dealer offered us barley grains sufficient for his own use. We ate that much on that day. And during the full three months of the *vas* season, the horse dealers continued making that offering in like manner.[109] This, O monks, is one *karma*.

XIa. "In the past, at one time I was born in the Mallava (wrestler) *kula*. Hearing that another wrestler had come to my

---

105. In fact, rice made of *äl* paddy is preferable to eat over barley grains. *Pkp* would have the slander be directed at disciples, in the plural, of the Buddha Phussa. For a parallel to this story in Buddhist Sanskrit Hīnayāna tradition, see the story of one of the Buddha's previous births in the Gilgit manuscripts' account of "Buddha at Vairambha" as recounted by Nalinaksha Dutt, 1947, p. 5.

106. Māra is generally regarded as the personification of Death, the Evil One, the Tempter, and is the Buddhist counterpart of the Devil or Principle of Destruction. See *DPPN*, vol. 2, pp. 611–20.

107. Verañjā is a town in which the Buddha once spent the rainy season at the invitation of the Brahman Verañja. Regarding Verañjā, and the above story, see *DPPN*, vol. 2, pp. 929–30.

108. Uttarāṅga is Uttarapatha, the northern division of Jambudīpa, or India. Its extent is not entirely clear. The chief divisions included in this territory are mentioned in Pāli literature as Kasmīra-Gandhāra and Kamboja. This region was famous from very early times for its horses and horse-dealers, and horses were brought down for sale from there to such cities as Benares. See *DPPN*, vol. 1, p. 363.

109. For a parallel to this story in Buddhist Sanskrit Hīnayāna tradition, see in the Gilgit manuscripts the account of the "Buddha at Vairambha" as recounted by Nalinaksha Dutt, 1947, pp. 4–5.

place, I went to him, saying, 'So, you came to wrestle with me. Ha!'. I closed the door, pinched him down, and wrung his back.

XIb. "As a result of that *karma*, now as Buddha I suffered from backache. Now, (although) I have the strength of ten crores of elephants of the *kālava* species,[110] a master wrestler named Pukkusa tackled me firmly. The elder Ānanda, at my request, went to him and released me from his grip.[111] O monks, this is another *karma*.

XIIa. "In the past, I was born in a certain family and was practicing medicine. I treated a certain wealthy merchant with purgation. When I noticed that he was not going to pay me, I was angry and gave him some incompatible medicine, thereby causing him to suffer.[112]

XIIb. "Because of that demeritorious deed, in this birth as Buddha, when I was living in Rājagaha I was greatly suffering from indigestion and Jīvaka gave me some medicine and made me purge thirty times.[113] This, O monks, is one *karma*.

---

110. This is the lowest of ten species of elephants, having the strength of ten men.

111. Pukkusa was a Mallarājaputta, a prince of the wrestlers. See *DPPN*, vol. 2, p. 214. This story is not related in *DPPN*. It is told here in the Sinhalese text only.

112. In the corresponding Pāli verse, it is the son of the merchant who is treated. Also, it is not noted there that the Buddha in his previous life saw that the merchant was not going to pay, or that he gave him an incompatible medicine because of this.

113. Jīvaka, or Jīvaka-Komārabhacca, was a celebrated physician. He was the son of Sālavatī, a courtesan of Rājagaha. See *DPPN*, vol. 1, pp. 957–58. *DPPN* relates that once when the Buddha was ill, Jīvaka found it necessary to administer a purge, and he had fat rubbed into the Buddha's body and gave him a handful of lotuses to smell. Jīvaka was away when the purgative acted, and suddenly remembered that he had omitted to ask the Buddha to bathe in warm water to complete the cure. The Buddha read his thoughts and bathed as required. See *Mahāvagga* 8, 1, 30–33 of the *Vinaya Piṭaka* for this story (*Vin*, vol. 1, pp. 278–80; *VT*, vol. 2, pp. 191–93). The corresponding Pāli verse to the Sinhalese text here just notes that the Buddha had diarrhea, or perhaps dysentery, as a consequence of his earlier deed. The Pāli

XIIIa. "In the past, I was born as the Brahman Jotipāla during the time of the Buddha Kāśyapa (P. Kassapa).[114] I was not aware of the existence of this Buddha and for the first time I heard of this Buddha from my friend, a potter named Ghaṭīkāra.[115] Not believing my friend's words. I said: 'There is no Buddha.' Then the potter said: 'Yesterday I was to the Buddha Kāśyapa and I listened to him preaching. Today I thought of attending one of his discourses again in your company.' Even then the Brahman did not believe him and said: 'You are telling lies. The Buddha, supreme in the three worlds, is indeed a rare phenomenon. How can there be such a great being at this time? ...' Thus I denied the existence of Buddha.[116]

XIIIb. "Due to the evil deed of saying through ignorance that the omniscient Buddha Kāśyapa was not a Buddha, now

---

text reads that the Buddha suffered from *pakkhandikā*, which clearly means "diarrhea" or "dysentery". In the *Vinaya Piṭaka* passage, the Buddha suffers from *dosā* "disorder of the three humours". *UP*, as against *BN*, as well reads that the Buddha suffered from diarrhea, not indigestion. The idea of indigestion or diarrhea being caused by a previous *karma* corresponds to the Ayurvedic concept of some diseases arising due to *karma*. See the essay on "Nosology in Ayurveda: Data from a Pāli Canonical Text" in J. Liyanaratne, 1999, pp. 72–83. This paper treats the names and classification of diseases (nosology) in the *Girimānanda Sutta* of the *Aṅguttara Nikāya* and in its commentary in the *Monorathapūraṇī*, and compares this to the classical Ayurvedic theories of Caraka, Suśruta, and Vāgbhaṭa.

114. Kassapa was the twenty-fourth Buddha, the third of the present aeon, and one of the seven Buddhas mentioned in the Pāli canon. He is the Buddha immediately preceding Gotama. His body was twenty cubits high and he lived for 20,000 years. See *DPPN*, vol. 1, pp. 544–47.

115. Ghaṭīkāra was a potter of Vehaliṅga who looked after his blind parents in the time of Kassapa Buddha. At the time of Ghaṭīkāra the Bodhisatta was a young Brahman named Jotipāla. See *DPPN*, vol. 1, pp. 823–24. See also *DPPN*, vol. 1, p. 545 and vol. 1, p. 971.

116. Jotipāla was the Bodhisatta born as a Brahman of Vehaliṅga in the time of Kassapa Buddha. The insulting remark made by Jotipāla regarding Kassapa Buddha led to Gotama, in his last life, having to practice austerities for a longer period than did the other Buddhas. The memory of what he did as Jotipāla was one of the things that made the Buddha smile. See *DPPN*, vol. 1, p. 971.

in this birth I found it difficult to attain Buddhahood. Whereas other Buddhas became such after seven days or a few months after their renunciation, as for me, I became Buddha only after a full six years (of exertion) in the province of Uruvelā.[117] This, O monks, is one *karma*.

XIV. "After becoming Buddha, I went to a Brahman village called Pañcasālā[118] to beg for alms. Due to an evil deed of a previous life, the people of that village were possessed of Māra and I was deprived of obtaining even a morsel of food (literally, 'even rice and betel'). So, I left that village on an empty stomach and said, "Ye Māra, today I spend the day in joy like the radiant Brahmans." This, O monks, is one *karma*.[119]

XV. "Again in the past I had done another demeritorious deed. Because of that, at the time I was dwelling in the village called Beluva, I surrendered my life to Māra and was lying down with abdominal hemorrhaging.[120] Then, the great king of gods,

---

117. Uruvelā was a locality on the banks of the Nerañjarā, in the neighborhood of the *bodhi*-tree at Buddhagayā. Here, the Bodhisatta practiced during six years the most severe penances. His companions were the Pañcavaggiya monks who, however, left him when he relaxed the severity of his austerities. The place chosen by the Bodhisatta for his penances was called Senānigama. See *DPPN*, vol. 1, pp. 435–36.

118. Pañcasālā was a Brahman village of Magadha where the Buddha begged alms after becoming Buddha. The Buddha received no alms due to Māra, by whom the people were possessed. The story is told in the *Piṇḍa Sutta* of the *Saṃyutta Nikāya*. See the text as in *S*, vol. 1, pp. 113–14, and the translation of *KS*, vol. 1, pp. 143–44. See *DPPN*, vol. 2, p. 105.

119. *UP* omits this story in Sinhalese, but includes in its place the Pāli verse referred to in *BN*. There is no corresponding Pāli text for this story in *Pkp*.

120. Beluva was a village near Vesāli where the Buddha spent his last *vassa* (rainy season retreat). He fell grievously ill during this period, but, by a great effort of will, overcame his sickness. He felt it would not be right for him to die without addressing his followers and taking leave of the Order. This is one of several times when Māra approached the Buddha and requested him to die, we are told. During this sickness in Beluva, Sakka ministered to the Buddha, waiting on

Sak (Skt. Śakra, P. Sakka),[121] removed the blood oozing from my body and attended on me. This, O monks, is one *karma.*[122]

XVIa. "At one time, in the great *Vessantara Jātaka,*[123] when the two children were given to the Brahman Jūjaka,[124]

---

him and carrying on his head the Buddha's stools when he suffered from accute dysentery. See *DPPN*, vol. 2, pp. 313–14, esp. p.313, n. 2, and under the discussion of Māra, vol. 2, p. 618.

121. Sakka is almost always spoken of as chief, or king, of the gods. He rules over the heavenly sphere Tāvatiṃsa, a heaven of the lower plane. His palace is Vejayanta, and his chariot bears the same name. He was considered by the early Buddhists to be a god of high character, kindly and just, but not perfect, and not very intelligent. Sakka's devotion to the Buddha and his religion is proverbial. When the Bodhisatta cut off his hair and threw it into the sky, Sakka took it and deposited it in the Cūḷāmaṇi-cetiya. He was present near the *bodhi*-tree, blowing his Vijayuttara-saṅkha, when Māra arrived to prevent the Buddha from reaching enlightenment. And so forth. Sakka appears as the guardian of moral law in the world. When wickedness is rampant among men, or kings become unrighteous, he appears among them to frighten them so that they may do good instead of evil. T. W. Rhys Davids has suggested that Sakka and Indra, with whom he shares many epithets, are independent conceptions. See *DPPN*, vol. 2, pp. 957–65.

122. This story is referred to incompletely and in very corrupt Sinhalese text in *UP*. It figures as no. XIV in my numbering of stories as in that manuscript. There is no corresponding Pāli text for this story in *Pkp.*

123. For the story of the *Vessantara Jātaka* (No. 547), see *DPPN*, vol. 2, pp. 594–97.

124. Jūjaka was a Brahman of Dunniviṭṭha in Kaliṅga. He was given a young maiden in repayment for a debt, but because she was praised for her virtues, the other wives in the village grew jealous of her and mocked her as an old man's darling. Thereafter she refused to go to the village well, and suggested that Jūjaka should obtain as slaves the children of Vessantara, then living as an ascetic in Vaṅkagiri. After many adventures Jūjaka found Vessantara, was allowed to have the two children, Jāli and Kaṇhājinā, and having tied their hands together, took them away. After he had traveled sixty leagues, the gods led him to Jetuttara where the children's grandfather reigned as king. The king bought the children back from Jūjaka at a very great price and gave him choice foods to eat. Jūjaka, having over-eaten and being unable to digest the food, died on the spot. He is identified with Devadatta. See *DPPN*, vol. 1, pp. 961–62.

the two children, crying, saw a moment of inattention of the haggard Brahman and tearing away the creepers that tied their hands, came running back. The Brahman chased behind them, and for a second time the two children were given over to him, hands tied. Then, seeing the wicked Brahman taking away the children and beating them with a stick under my own eyes, and also seeing the children looking back (at me) crying and worshipping me with hands placed on their heads, I became angry with the Brahman. Overwhelmed with sorrow I thought, 'This wretched Brahman is beating my children even in front of me. Should I strike him with my sword?' With that thought, I looked at the sword. I stared angrily at the uncouth Brahman's face thinking as to whether I should tie him up with a creeper. With that thought, I looked at a creeper. Further, when I enjoyed riches as a great monarch as in the case of the *Vessantara Jātaka*, I gave away innumerable times from Buddhahood up to *parinirvāṇa* jewels of sons like Jāliya (P. Jāli),[125] daughters like Kṛṣṇajinā (P. Kaṇhājinā),[126]

---

125. Jāli was the son of Vessantara and Maddī, and brother of Kaṇhājinā. He and his sister were given to Jūjaka as slaves, but were later rescued by the intervention of Sakka. Jāli led the army that brought Vessantara back from his hermitage. He is identified with Rāhula, the only son of Gotama Buddha. The gift of Jāli as a slave is considered one of the greatest sacrifices made by the Bodhisatta. See *DPPN*, vol. 1, pp. 954.

126. Kaṇhājinā was the daughter of Vessantara and Maddī. When Vessantara retired to the forest, his wife and children accompanied him to Vaṅkagiri. Later, both Kaṇhājinā and her brother Jāli were given to Jūjaka as slaves and were ill-treated by him. For sixty leagues they traveled with him, led and guarded by the gods, till they came to the court of their grandfather Sañjaya, king of Sivi, and there they were released, Kaṇhājinā's price being one hundred elephants, one hundred male and female slaves, etc. The children afterwards rejoined their parents and lived happily at the court. Kaṇhājinā is identified with Uppalavaṇṇā, the great *therī* who was one of the two chief women disciples of the Buddha. See *DPPN*, vol. 1, pp. 503–504.

dainty queens like Queen Madrī (P. Maddī).[127] After having practiced generosity in that manner, that day I became cross at the Brahman's rudeness, like sowing seeds in a good field at an inauspicious time.[128]

XVIb. "As a result, when I was seated under the *bodhi*-tree to attain Buddhahood, Vasavartī Māra (P. Vasavattī)[129] assumed a form with 500 fearful heads, a thousand red eyes like red balls, a thousand fearful teeth coming out of his cheeks, and stared angrily at me. Because I thought of tying up the Brahman, Māra's three daughters came to tie me up with garlands.[130] O monks, this is another *karma*.

---

127. Maddī was the wife of Vessantara. When Vessantara went into exile, she, with her two children, Jāli and Kaṇhājinā, accompanied him. At Vaṅkagiri she and the children occupied one of the hermitages provided for them by Vissakamma, at Sakka's orders. While she was getting fruit and leaves, Jūjaka obtained from Vessantara the two children as slaves. Maddī the previous night had had a dream warning her of this, but Vessantara had consoled her. When she came back from her quest for food later than usual, the gods having contrived to detain her, she found the children missing and searched for them throughout the night. It was at dawn the next day, on her recovery from a deathlike swoon, that Vessantara told her of the gift of the children, describing the miracles that had attended the gift and showing how they presaged that he would reach enlightenment. Maddī, understanding, rejoiced herself in the gift. The next day, Sakka appeared in the guise of a Brahman and asked Vessantara to give him Maddī as his slave. Seeing him hesitate, Maddī urged him to let her go, saying that she belonged to him to do as he would with her. The gift was made and accepted by Sakka. He then, however, gave her back with praises of Vessantara and Maddī. Maddī is identified with Rāhulamātā, Rāhula's mother and Gotama's wife. See *DPPN*, vol. 2, pp. 434–35.

128. This narration does not appear in *UP*. There is also no corresponding Pāli text for this story in *Pkp*. In *BN* there is the incorrect reading, Jūtaka, for Jūjaka.

129. Vasavattī is a name given to Māra. See *DPPN*, vol. 2, p. 844.

130. This narration does not appear in *UP*. There is no corresponding Pāli text for this incident in *Pkp*.

XVIIa. "When I was perfecting the *pāramitās*, there were two streets in a village not far away from the city of Baranäs (P. Bārāṇasī, Eng. Benares).[131] There were two families there. In one of them, there were two sons. The younger brother was the Bodhisatta. The Bodhisatta's brother was married to a daughter brought home from another family. The Bodhisatta, not having a house of his own, continued to live with his brother. One day, sweet pastries were prepared in the house. Dividing them into three shares, the couple ate two shares and kept the third for the Bodhisatta who had gone to the forest for some purpose. Then, a *paccekabuddha* living in the Gandhamādana Mountain,[132] going on his alms round from door to door, came and stood in front of that house. The couple saw the *paccekabuddha* at their doorstep and not having anything else in the house to be offered, the wife of the Bodhisatta's brother thought, 'Pastries could be prepared later for the person who has gone to the forest.' And she offered the Bodhisatta's share to the *paccekabuddha*. Then, when the Bodhisatta returned home from the forest, the woman said, 'We kept a share of pastries for you. But I offered it to a *paccekabuddha* who came begging for alms. Be happy (literally, 'make your mind serene').' When he heard that, the Bodhisatta thought, 'What made you eat your share and offer mine?' Being angered, he ran after the *paccekabuddha*, stared at him angrily, and seized the pastries in his bowl.[133]

---

131. Bārāṇasī (Benares) was the capital of Kāsi *janapada*. It was one of the four places of pilgrimage for the Buddhists. Bārāṇasī was an important center of trade and industry. There was direct trade between there and Sāvatthi, and between there and Takkasilā. In the past, Bārāṇasī was the birthplace of Kassapa Buddha. See *DPPN*, vol. 2, pp. 274–77.

132. For Gandhamādana, see above under the text's introductory statement that the Buddha confessed this text at Anotatta Lake.

133. This story is from the *Kusa Jātaka* (No. 531). See *SBFB*, vol. 5, pp. 149–50 for the story. The story is related in the *Kusa Jātaka* as an explanation of King Kusa's ugliness. An additional incident not related here but connected with this story explains why Pabhāvatī wanted nothing to do with Kusa at first. This narration is not given in *UP*. There is no corresponding Pāli text for this story in *Pkp*.

XVIIb. "As a result of that evil deed, now in my last birth as Buddha, when I went alone to the city of Sävät (P. Sāvatthi)[134] to beg alms, there was a certain woman who used to keep a spoonful of rice to be offered to the great *thera* Mahā-Kāśyapa (P. Mahā-Kassapa).[135] That day, I went first on the alms round. Seeing me, (the woman) taking me to be the *thera*, offered the spoonful of rice into my bowl. Then, while going back to the house, she saw the *thera* coming after me. Perturbed at that and saying, 'I offered my spoonful of rice to someone else,' she came running after me, the Buddha, shouting, 'Wait monk, wait!' She seized the spoonful of rice put into my bowl.[136] O monks, this is another *karma*.

XVIII. "Then again, in this life, while I was residing in a *jeta* grove I became sick from the three humors. At that time a great *thera* named Upavāṇa[137] and a Brahman named Devahita[138]

---

134. Sāvatthi was the capital town of Kosala in India, and one of the six great Indian cities during the lifetime of the Buddha. See *DPPN*, vol. 2, pp. 1126–27.

135. Kassapa Thera was the son of an Udicca Brahman of Sāvatthi who died when Kassapa was still young. Having heard the Buddha preach at Jetavana, he entered the First Fruit of the Path and, with his mother's leave, became a monk. Some time later, wishing to accompany the Buddha on a tour after the rains, he went to bid his mother farewell. Her admonition to him on that occasion helped him to win insight and become an *arahant*. He is probably identical with Sereyyaka Thera of the *Apadāna*. See *DPPN*, vol. 1, p. 547.

136. I have not been able to locate this incident in the Pāli canon. This story is not given in *UP*. There is no corresponding Pāli text for this incident in *Pkp*.

137. Upavāṇa was a great *thera*. Once when the Buddha was attacked by cramp, Upavāṇa, with the help of his lay friend Devahita, obtained hot water and suitable medicines, with which the ailment was healed. See *DPPN*, vol. 1, pp. 399–400.

138. Devahita was a Brahman of Sāvatthi. Once when the Buddha was ill with cramp and desired hot water Upavāṇa obtained from Devahita hot water and molasses, which he sent on a pingo by a serving man. Hot fomentations and the administering of molasses cured the Buddha's complaint. Devahita came later to the Buddha, and after

heard about my illness, came to me and nursed me in order to acquire merit. This Brahman bathed me in medicated water and gave me honey mixed with hot water to drink.[139] Thereupon, the disorder of the three humours subsided. This, O monks, is one *karma*.[140]

XIX. "Further, a demon named Sūciroma (P. Sūciloma, Suciloma, Sinh. Sūciroma, Sūciloma)[141] living on a stone slab on the four stone pillars called Ṭaṃkitavadva (P. Ṭaṅkitamañca) in Magadha,[142] came running to me with the thought, 'I will prick

---

some conversation he was converted. The *Saṃyutta* commentary adds that Devahita earned his living from the provision of water heated on his row of ovens and of cosmetics for those who came to bathe. On hearing of the Buddha's illness, he gave to Upavāṇa a kind of treacle to be administered in water. See *DPPN*, vol. 1, pp. 1117–18.

139. Regarding the medicinal use of honey, see *Bhesajjamañjūsā* 6.73–81 (*Bhes*, pp. 105–106; *CM*, pp. 73–74). The *Bhesajjamañjūsā* is a 13th c. CE. Pāli medical work. It is the only known medical work written in Pāli.

140. *UP* gives the name of the *thera* as Mānava, and the name of the Brahman as Devagīta. *BN* also refers to the Brahman as Devagīta. The name was corrected on the basis of *DPPN*. This story figures as no. XV in my numbering of the stories as in *UP*. There is no corresponding Pāli text for this story in *Pkp*.

141. Sūciloma is a Yakkha the hairs of whose body resembled needles. Once, when the Buddha was at the Ṭaṅkitamañca in Gayā, which was the abode of Sūciloma, Sūciloma and his friend, Khara, happened to be passing by and Sūciloma, coming *UP* to the Buddha, bent his body against the Buddha's. The Buddha bent his body in the opposite direction, saying that contact with him was an evil thing. Then Sūciloma asked him a question regarding the origin of mental and emotional dispositions and the Buddha answered him. This is related in the *Sūciloma Sutta* of the *Sutta Nipāta*. See, for instance, Lord Robert Chalmers, 1932, pp. 66–69. See also *S*, vol. 1, pp. 207–208 and *KS*, vol. 1, pp. 264–66. See *DPPN*, vol. 2, p. 1180.

142. Magadha was one of the four chief kingdoms of India at the time of the Buddha, the others being Kosala, the kingdom of the Vaṃsas, and Avanti. During the early Buddhist period Magadha was an important political and commercial center, and was visited by people from all parts of northern India in search of commerce and learning. Magadha is identified with modern south Bihar. See *DPPN*, vol. 2, pp. 402–404.

and stick this monk with the iron needles that are hairs on my body.' O monks, this is another *karma*.[143]

XXa. "At one time, when I was born as the scholar Mahosadha[144] (as related in the) *Mahā-Ummagga Jātaka*, for the marriage of King Videha,[145] I went to see King Cūḷani-Brahmadatta[146] of the country called Uttarapañcāla[147] which was 400 *gāvutas* away[148] from the city of Miyuḷu (P. Mithilā)[149] and asked for stones to build houses for King Videha. For that purpose, when (we) started to break *UP* all houses without exception in that great city, forty-eight *gāvutas* long, the bribes given to save those houses were by measure nine crores of gold. Spending four crores and fifty out of that, I built palaces. And

---

143. *UP* begins by mentioning that this incident happened when the Buddha was living in Gayā. It then does not mention Magadha as in *BN*. This story figures as no. XVI in my numbering of the stories as in *UP*. There is no corresponding Pāli text for this story in *Pkp*. The town of Gayā was in the kingdom of Magadha. It lay on the road between the *bodhi*-tree and Benares. The Buddha stayed at Gayā on several occasions. See *DPPN*, vol. 1, p. 752.

144. Mahosadha was the Bodhisatta born as minister to King Vedeha. For his details and the story referred to here, see the *Mahā-Ummagga Jātaka* (No. 546). See *DPPN*, vol. 2, p. 594 and vol. 2, pp. 465–68, esp. pp. 466–67 for the story referred to here.

145. Vedeha was the personal name of the king of Mithilā, whose minister was Mahosadha. See *DPPN*, vol. 2, p. 922.

146. Cūḷani-Brahmadatta is the king of Uttarapañcāla in the *Mahā-Ummagga Jātaka*. See *DPPN*, vol. 1, p. 908 and vol. 1, p. 357, n. 4 under Uttarapañcāla.

147. Uttarapañcāla is given variously as the name of a city in the country of Kampilla, or as the name of a country whose capital was Kampilla. See *DPPN*, vol. 1, pp. 357–58 and vol. 2, p. 108 under Pañcāla.

148. 1 *gāvuta* = a little less than two miles.

149. Mithilā was the capital of the Videha country. It is generally identified with Janakapura, a small town within the Nepal border. In the Indian Epics, Mithilā is chiefly famous as the residence of King Janaka. See *DPPN*, vol. 2, p. 635.

because of that wealth that country was taken by force and the army of that country was spoiled.[150]

XXb. "As a result of that deed, when I was living in Jetavanārāma,[151] two monks of Ghositārāma who were versed in *vinaya* (monastic discipline) and *abhidhamma* (doctrine) (respectively) had an argument about an accusation relating to *vinaya*.[152] My attendants also split themselves into two sides. The nuns who were receiving advice from the two monks also split into two groups. Then the divinities who were patrons of the fourfold assembly of monks, nuns, lay male disciples, and lay female disciples took two separate sides. The celestial and earth-bound divinities of the two groups also took sides with the two groups. Seeing them, the divinities of the heavenly spheres of Caturmahārajika, Tāvatiṃsa, Yāma, Tusita, Nimmānarati, and Paranimmitavasavatti (the six divine abodes)[153] split into two groups. Then, not only that, even the Brahmapārisajja Brahma-realm (name of the lowest Rūpa-Brahmaloka) and up to the Akaniṭṭha Brahma-world, the sixteen Brahma-worlds also were divided.[154] And there was a very big conflict. Then

150. This story is not given in *UP*. There is no corresponding Pāli text for this story in *Pkp*.

151. For Jetavanārāma, see Jetavana referred to earlier. See *DPPN*, vol. 1, pp. 963–66 and p. 967.

152. Ghositārāma is a monastery in Kosambī. The Buddha often stayed there during his visits to Kosambī and numerous incidents are mentioned in the books in connection with the monastery. It was because of a dispute between two monks of the Ghositārāma, one expert in the *vinaya* and one in the *dhamma*, that the first schism arose in the Order, driving the Buddha himself to seek quiet in the Pārileyyaka forest. Even at other times the Buddha seems to have sought solitude in this forest during his sojourn at the Ghositārāma. See *DPPN*, vol. 1, pp. 829–31.

153. For this division see *PED*, p. 329a, bottom; W. Kirfel, 1920, p. 191 and p. 194.

154. For the various Brahma-worlds, sixteen being Rūpa-Brahmaloka, or worlds of form, and four above them being Arūpa-Brahmaloka, inhabited by *devas* who are incorporeal, see W. Kirfel, 1920, pp. 191–2 and p. 194.

the *saṅgha* (monastic community, or Order) also divided into two parties. Then I could not bring them into calmness, and I took my bowl and robes and went all alone to the forest called Rakkhita.[155] And during the time of three months that I was there, during the time of spring retreat, an elephant known as Pārileyya[156] helped me.[157] O monks, this is another *karma.*

XXIa. "At one time, Queen Talatā,[158] the mother of King Cūḷani-Brahmadatta of the *Mahā-Ummagga Jātaka*, his queen Nanda,[159] his son Prince Pañcālacaṇḍa,[160] and his daughter

---

155. Rakkhita-vanasaṇḍa is a forest tract near the village of Pārileyya. There the Buddha retired and lived at the foot of the Bhaddasāla when unable to settle the dispute among the Kosambī monks. The elephant Pārileyya lived there and waited upon the Buddha. It is said that the place derived its name from the fact that Pārileyya looked after the Buddha, guarding him throughout the night, wandering about the forest till dawn, a stick in his trunk, in order to ward off danger. See *DPPN*, vol. 2, p. 704.
156. Pārileyya, or Pārileyyaka, is the name of an elephant who, finding communal life distasteful, had left his herd and waited on the Buddha, ministering to all his needs when the Buddha left Ghositārāma alone and unattended after he found he could not persuade the Kosambī monks to refrain from quarrelling. The commentaries describe in vivid detail the perfect manner in which Pārileyya looked after the Buddha, omitting nothing, even to the extent of finding hot water for his bath. Pārileyyaka died of a broken heart when the Buddha left the forest, and was born in Tāvatiṃsa in a golden palace, thirty leagues high, where he came to be known as Pārileyyaka-devaputta. See *DPPN*, vol. 2, pp. 191–92.
157. This incident is not given in *UP*. There is no corresponding Pāli text for this incident in *Pkp.*
158. Talatādevī was the mother of Cūḷani-Brahmadatta, king of Pañcāla, her husband being Mahā Cūḷani. See *DPPN*, vol. 1, p. 998.
159. Nandādevī was the chief queen of Cūḷani-Brahmadatta, king of Pañcāla. She is identified with Yasassikā. See *DPPN*, vol. 2, p. 25 and vol. 2, p. 468. There is no separate listing for Yasassikā in *DPPN*.
160. Pañcālacaṇḍa was the son of Cūḷani-Brahmadatta. He was sent by Mahosadha to be kept as hostage to King Videha, when Cūḷani-Brahmadatta threatened to harm the latter. But Videha treated him like a younger brother. Pañcālacaṇḍī was sister to Pañcālacaṇḍa. See *DPPN*, vol. 2, p. 109.

Princess Pañcālacaṇḍī[161]—these four, I took as prisoners and gave them over to King Videha.[162]

XXIb. "Due to that evil deed, when I was living in Jetavanārāma my daughter Kṛṣṇajinā (P. Kaṇhājinā) who had become the great *therī* Upulvan (P. Uppalavaṇṇā)[163] used to sleep in a bed in a cell in the forest hermitage of Andhavana.[164] One day, she begged alms in the city of Sāvatthi and after the meal, was lying on the bed in the forest hermitage. Then the son of her uncle, who was a rich merchant, Ānanda,[165] already in

---

161. Pañcālacaṇḍī was the daughter of Cūḷani-Brahmadatta. Her marriage with King Videha, which was accomplished by the wisdom and diplomacy of Mahosadha, forms the main theme of the *Mahā-Ummagga Jātaka*. She bore a son to Videha, who succeeded him ten years after the marriage. Pañcālacaṇḍī is identified with the *therī* Sundarī-(Nandā). See *DPPN*, vol. 2, p. 110.

162. This incident is not given in *UP*. There is no corresponding Pāli text for this incident in *Pkp*.

163. Uppalavaṇṇā was a great *therī* and one of the two chief women disciples of the Buddha. Vessantara's daughter Kaṇhājinā is identified with her. The books give several episodes connected with Uppalavaṇṇā. Once a young man named Ānanda, who was her cousin and had been in love with her during her lay life, hid himself in her hut in Andhavana and, in spite of her protestations, deprived her of her chastity. From that time onwards, nuns were forbidden to live in Andhavana. See *DPPN*, vol. 1, pp. 418–21.

164. Andhavana was a grove to the south of Sāvatthi, one *gāvuta* away from the city. It was well guarded, and monks and nuns used to resort there in search of solitude. See *DPPN*, vol. 1, pp. 111–12.

165. Ānanda, called Māṇava in order to distinguish him from the others. He was a Brahman youth, maternal cousin to the *therī* Uppalavaṇṇā, with whom he had been in love when she was a laywoman. One day when Uppalavaṇṇā returned from her alms rounds to her hut in Andhavana, where she was living at the time, Ānanda-māṇava, who was hiding under her bed, jumped *UP* and seized her. In spite of her protestations and admonitions, he overcame her resistence by force and, having worked his will of her, went away. As if unable to endure his wickedness, the earth burst asunder and he was swallowed *UP* in Avīci. In order that such assaults should not be repeated, Pasenadi Kosala erected, at the Buddha's suggestion, a residence for the nuns

love with her when she was a laywoman, had sexual intercourse with her.[166] O monks, this is another *karma.*

XXIIa. "In the war of *dhamma* with the Brahman Kevaṭṭa[167] in the city of Miyuḷu (P. Mithilā) in the same *Mahā-Ummagga Jātaka*, I, as the scholar Mahosadha, took (Kevaṭṭa) by the neck with one hand, by the hip with the other, and rubbed his face on the ground till his chin, lips, cheeks, nose, and forehead were bloodied as if smeared with lac. Then, when I pushed him away by the neck, he went and fell several *ratanas* away[168] like a leaf blown off by the wind.[169]

XXIIb. "As a result of that evil deed, after forty-five years of Buddhahood my tooth relics were beaten up on an anvil and thrown into a pit of excrement.[170] O monks, this is another *karma.*"

End of the *Detiskarmmaya.*

---

within the city gates, and henceforth they lived only within the precincts of the city. See *DPPN*, vol. 1, p. 272.

166. This account is not given in *UP*. There is no corresponding Pāli text for this narration in *Pkp*. In *BN* the name Ānanda is incorrectly given as Nanda.

167. Kevaṭṭa was the chaplain of Cūḷani-Brahmadatta, king of Uttarapañcāla. He was wise and learned, and clever in device. The king followed his counsel and conquered all the territories of India except that of King Videha of Mithilā. When at last Brahmadatta laid siege to Mithilā, Kevaṭṭa was responsible for the details of the siege. But his plans were upset by Mahosadha who, though his junior in age, was far wiser. See *DPPN*, vol. 1, pp. 666–67.

168. In common usage, 1 *ratana* = eighteen *aṅgulas*, finger-breadths, or inches.

169. This is an abridged translation of the sentence, which is a graphic description of Kevaṭṭa's predicament. This story is not given in *UP*. There is no corresponding Pāli text for this story in *Pkp*.

170. Regarding the Buddha's tooth relics, see the *Dāṭhāvaṃsa*, an 11th c. CE. composition by Dhammakīrti. See also the essay on "The Tooth of the Buddha" in Harvey Rachlin, 2000, pp. 3–11, esp. p. 7, which refers in brief to the incidents mentioned in the text here. This narration is not given in *UP*. There is no corresponding Pāli text for this narration in *Pkp*.

UP has a different story regarding the schism than the one given in *BN*. In the sequence of numbering established for *UP* alone, this would be no. XVII—though it corresponds to *BN*, no. XXa and XXb. The account is as follows:

XVII. "While I was living in Veḷuvanārāma,[171] Devadatta, the great elder, caused dissention in the community of monks by taking away the 500 Vajjiputta (P. Vajjiputtakā) monks.[172] This is another *karma* of mine.[173]

---

171. Veḷuvana was a park near Rājagaha, the pleasure garden of Bimbisāra. The king bestowed it on the Buddha and the fraternity. This was the first *ārāma*, or park, accepted by the Buddha. The Buddha spent several *vassas*, or rainy season retreats, at Veḷuvana. During one of the Buddha's stays at Veḷuvana, Sāriputta and Moggallāna brought back the 500 monks whom Devadatta had enticed to secede from the Order. See *DPPN*, vol. 2, pp. 936–39, esp. p. 937.

172. Vajjiputtakā, or Vajjiputtiyā, is the name of a large group of monks belonging to the Vajjian clan. Vajjī is the kingdom of the Licchavīs. Vesāli was its capital. The first great schism of the Buddhist Order arose in Vajjī one century after the Buddha's death, when these monks brought forward Ten Points as being permissible for members of the Order. The orthodox monks refused to agree to these points, and one of their leaders publicly condemned the action of the Vajjiputtakās. This is foreshadowed during the Buddha's life by 500 newly ordained monks from Vesāli described as Vajjiputtakā seceding from the Order and joining Devadatta, though they were later brought back by Sāriputta and Moggallāna. Buddhaghosa identifies the later heretics as belonging to the same party as the earlier group of 500. See *DPPN*, vol. 2, pp. 812–13, esp. 812, n. 1, and pp. 813–15; also *DPPN*, vol. 1, p. 1109; vol. 2, p. 545; vol. 2, p. 937; and vol. 2, pp. 1111–12.

173. There is no corresponding Pāli text for this narration in *Pkp*. That there is in this location, placed last in the text of *UP*, mention of the 500 monks who seceded from the Order at Devadatta's instigation but who were brought back into the Order by Sāriputta and Moggallāna perhaps echoes at the end of the Sinhalese text here the beginning frame story of the Buddhist Sanskrit *Anavataptagāthā* and *Sthaviragāthā*. This latter involves Sāriputta (Skt. Śāriputra) and Moggallāna (Skt. Maudgalyāyana). See Marcel Hofinger, 1954, pp. 181–92.

There then follows a summation, which is not found in *BN*. As noted above, this corresponds to *Pkp*, vss. 31–32, and 33. This summation in *UP* translates:

"I attained Buddhahood under a *bodhi*-tree which brings supreme knowledge and takes me to the supreme city of Nibbāna. Thereby, I caused twenty-four *asaṅkheyyas* of people (*i.e.*, innumerable people) to attain Nibbāna. Whatever demeritorious deeds I have done before through my weaknesses, I had done before. As a result of that I had acquired demeritorious *karmas*. All that ripened in this last birth as Buddha." He told this to the monks. He said: "Monks, at this moment I do not have beneficial consequences of my meritorious deeds (each day) nor do I have evil consequences occurring in the future. I do not have any torments (P. *santāpa*) even in the future. I have exhausted both *puṇya* (P. *puñña*, merit) and *pāpa* (sin). I have abandoned torment. I am devoid of sorrow. I am devoid of turbulence. I am devoid of the fourfold *āśravas* (P. *āsava*, intoxicant).[174] I am devoid of sickness. I am devoid of illness. I am devoid of *upadravas* (P. *upaddava*, distress or misfortune). I am devoid of illness. I have attained nectar immutable *mahānirvāṇa* (P. *mahānibbāna*). Thus I have vanquished my enemies, namely *kleśas* (P. *kilesa*, defilement; or depravity, lust). Therefore I have the names ... (various epithets of Buddha)."

So Buddha described his *pubbakarma* (P. *pubbakamma*, previous deeds). All these past *karmas* had their consequences just as you pay your debts. So he gave a discourse of these past actions, namely *karma apadānapāli*, *karmas* that he had done during his life as Bodhisatta which, had their consequences. This is the end of this discourse called *Detiskarma padārthayi.*

174. The fourfold *āsavas*, as noted earlier, are sensuality, rebirth (lust of life), speculation, and ignorance.

Summary of the *Detiskarma padārthayi* (*BN* and *UP*) and Its Relationship to the *Pubbakammapiloti* (*Pkp*)

An outline of *BN* shows how perfectly balanced the organization of this text is. Even in the shorter *UP*, the text remains perfectly balanced. In the following outline, the numbering of the extra material in *UP* beyond the scope of *Pkp* is placed in brackets following the numbering of this material as in *BN*. The outline follows:

Iab.	Thirst. [Craving.]
IIab.	
IIIab.	Trouble with women (virtue doubted). [Trouble with un-virtuous women.]
IVab.	
Vab.	
VIab.	Trouble with Devadatta. [Trouble with unvirtuous man.]
VIIab.	
VIIIab.	Sickness (external).
IXab.	Personal harm (harm to family), and Sickness (congenital).
Xab.	Difficulty in religion (alms).
XIab.	Personal harm (harm to self), and Sickness (congenital).
XIIab.	Sickness (internal).
XIIIab.	Difficulty in religion (austerities). [Difficulty obtaining Buddhahood.]
XIV.	[Related Pāli verse inserted.] [Difficulty in religion (alms).]
XV. [XIV.]	Trouble with Māra. [Sickness (internal).]

XVIab.	[Personal harm (due to unwholesome thought).]
XVIIab.	Difficulty in religion (alms).
XVIII. [XV.]	Sickness (from the three humours).
XIX. [XVI.]	Personal harm (harm from demon to self).
XXab. [XVII.]	Difficulty in religion (schism).*
XXIab.	Personal harm (harm to Buddha's daughter from a previous life, now a *therī*).
XXIIab.	Personal harm (harm to Buddha's tooth relics).

* *BN* and *UP* each have different stories regarding the schism.

It is interesting to note that many of the added stories of misfortune in the Buddha's life, not found in the *Apadāna* account, have no antecedent actions noted. This is an indication that, as J. S. Walters noted, the antecedent incidents have no parallels in Theravāda tradition.[175] Their only source in Theravāda tradition is *Pkp*.

Note that all of the extra stories in *UP* are without antecedent actions. This is true also of the extra story in *BN*, the presence of which in *UP* is hinted at only by its inclusion of the Pāli verse from the *Piṇḍa Sutta* to which this story refers. *UP*, as noted, does not contain the story in Sinhalese.

Of the additional extra stories in *BN*, one gives an antecedent action from the *Vessantara Jātaka* and three give antecedent actions from the *Mahā-Ummagga Jātaka*. The sources of these antecedent actions are stated in the Sinhalese text. The antecedent action of the other additional story (XVIIa) was traced to the *Kusa Jātaka*.

Both this, and the fact that the story of schism with antecedent action from the *Mahā-Ummagga Jātaka* in *BN* is different from that of schism without antecedent given in *UP*, suggest that *BN* is a further expansion of the tradition represented in *UP*. Perhaps indicating that this is a further expansion of the textual tradition as well is that the additional

175. J. S. Walters, 1990, p. 78.

stories in *BN* are lengthy when compared to the stories of *UP*. Also, the last story in *BN* contradicts the summation of *UP* in that it notes a *kamma*'s effect occurring after the Buddha's *parinibbāna*. The summation in *UP* clearly states, "at this moment I do not have beneficial consequences of my meritorious deeds (each day) nor do I have the evil consequences occurring in the future. I do not have any torments even in the future." *UP* itself represents an expansion of the tradition represented in *Pkp*. To be emphasized is that as can be seen in the outline of the texts, the expansions are well structured.

Also to be emphasized is the perfect balance of *Pkp*. Three stories of the Buddha's trouble with unvirtuous women are followed by three stories of the Buddha's trouble with an unvirtuous man, Devadatta. Then follow six other stories of the Buddha's difficulties, also perfectly organized. The initial additional story found in Thai manuscripts, and in *UP* and *BN*, frames this all perfectly.

The Northern Buddhist Versions

The corresponding text in the *Sthaviragāthā* from the *Bhaiṣajyavastu* of the *Mūlasarvāstivāda Vinaya*, and in the Sarvāstivādin *Anavataptagāthā*, is given in parallel Tibetan text and in parallel German translations from Chinese texts side-by-side with the corresponding Pāli text by *AS*.[176] A German translation of the Tibetan text follows in *AS*.[177] This material recounts only ten *karmas*. Omitted are the second and third stories regarding Devadatta as in the Pāli material, and the extra first verses as found in Thai manuscripts of the Pāli text and in our Sinhalese manuscripts here. *AS* includes these Pāli verses nevertheless, and translates in brackets those treating Devadatta along with its translation of the Tibetan text. The Buddhist Sanskrit text here is, as noted, not preserved except for a very few partly preserved verses toward the end of the *Anavataptagāthā* in the Turfan manuscripts.[178] It would seem that the ordering of the stories in the Tibetan and Chinese material is the same as in the Pāli material. The Gilgit manuscripts, however, contain a Buddhist Sanskrit prose summary which follows its missing verses and which is preserved in part only.[179] The prose account is missing both beginning and end. *AS* does not discuss the Gilgit manuscripts' version of our text as reflected in this summary. To be noticed here is that the ordering of incidents in this is different from that of the Pāli *Apadāna* text and the Sinhalese text. It is closer to the ordering of the Mahāyāna *Bodhisattvāvadānakalpalatā* (hence, *Av-klp*).

176. *AS*, pp. 204–208 and pp. 208–43.

177. *AS*, pp. 244–48.

178. See *AS*, p. 208, p. 239, p. 241.

179. Nalinaksha Dutt, 1947, pp. 28–29

The Mahāyāna Version: Chapter 50 of the *Bodhisattvāvadānakalpalatā* (*Av-klp*)

The corresponding Mahāyāna Buddhist text is the *Daśakarmmaplutyavadāna*, chapter 50 in the 11th c. CE. Kashmirian poet Kṣemendra's *Av-klp* as published in Sanskrit and Tibetan by Sarat Chandra Das and Paṇḍit Hari Mohan Vidyābhūshaṇa.[180] This account, as in the Buddhist Sanskrit Hīnayāna accounts, only recounts ten *karmas*.

Perhaps seven of the *karmas* discussed are the same as those in the Pāli and Sinhalese texts, but with different details. Thus the story of Munāli is here told more fully of Mṛṇāla, and the story regarding Jotipāla and Kassapa is abbreviated simply stating that in an earlier existence the Buddha spoke ill of a certain Pudgala (perhaps, of *pudgala*, according to one of the interpretations). The former birth as a physician who purged the son of a wealthy merchant in the Pāli text, the wealthy merchant himself in the Sinhalese text, is told here with more details and providing personal names. Similarly, in the story of brothers of two mothers, one of whom killed the other for the sake of wealth, more detail and names are provided. While the incident is related to a similar result, Devadatta is not mentioned in the Mahāyāna text.

The scandal involving Sundarī is here related to a different earlier deed than in the Pāli and Sinhalese texts. The story of Mṛṇāla, which one would expect to be connected to the scandal involving Sundarī, simply refers to false charges being brought against the Buddha by a woman or women. The introduction to the stories, though, clearly mentions Cañcā.[181] Also, the explanation for the Buddha eating barley in Verajjā for three months—a town and a duration not mentioned in the Mahāyāna text—appears to develop the Buddhist Sanskrit Hīnayāna tellings of this very differently than the Sinhalese account in simple Pāli text.

---

180. Sarat Chandra Das and Paṇḍit Hari Mohan Vidyābhūshaṇa, 1888–1918, vol. 2, pp. 2–43.

181. Cañcā = Pāli Ciñca, regarding which see below.

Two of the *karmas*, the second and third, have no correspondences in the Pāli and Sinhalese material discussed here. They are reflected in the Buddhist Sanskrit Hīnayāna texts, though. The second is reflected in the Tibetan and Chinese translations of the Buddhist Sanskrit Hīnayāna texts. The third is found in three of the few partially preserved Sanskrit verses in the Turfan manuscripts.[182]

Interestingly, in both the Mahāyāna tradition and in the Pāli tradition there is a beginning statement which mentions on the one hand the sewing of a monk's tunic, and on the other hand a little piece of cloth being given to a forest monk.[183] The Mahāyāna tradition can clearly be traced back to the beginning of the *Sthaviragāthā*.[184] Perhaps the symbolism here is a comparison of one's *kamma* with one's garb, and its threads.

Kṣemendra uses the stories as a medium to insert proverbs and proverbial wisdom, which greatly expands the length of some of the stories. He also expands some of the stories through dialogue. Other stories, on the other hand, remain in verses of limited length only.

This text has been retold in or translated into English several times with slightly different details each time.[185]

---

182. See *AS*, p. 241 for text.

183. The former appears in the Mahāyāna tradition here. See the Tibetan retelling of Giuseppe Tucci below. The latter appears in the Thai tradition and the Sinhalese tradition of *BN*.

184. See Marcel Hofinger, 1954, pp. 181–82.

185. It was first retold by Rājendralāla Mitra, 1882, pp. 57–58. It appeared in translation by two hands, identified as "B." (pp. 19–22) and as Pandit Ananda Prasād Sarasvatī (pp. 22–25), in *Journal of the Buddhist Text and Research Society, Calcutta* (hence, *JBTRS*) 1.4 (1893): 19–25. Text followed on pp. 9–20 of a following section of Sanskrit text alone. (A number of legends from the *Av-klp* by Kṣemendra are translated by various hands in *JBTRS* 1–7 [1893–1906]. Four metrical translations published there of four of the *pallavas* [nos. 65, 51, 9, 8] were published separately in Nobin Chandra Das, 1895.) It was next retold from Tibetan text by Giuseppe Tucci, 1949, vol. 2, pp. 489–92. This retelling was reprinted in Sharada Rani, 1977, serial no. 16, woodcut number R-15. Finally it was retold more recently,

That *Pkp* and the *Av-klp* 50 were parallel, but not quite identical texts, was pointed out first by *CPD*.[186] This text was also referred to in passing in *AS*.[187] Five verses of text from *Av-klp* 50 were also given in *AS*.[188]

This text is given below as recounted by Rājendralāla Mitra. If a *karma* is related much more fully or with significantly different details by Jayanti Chattopadhyay, the fuller account, or the account with different details, follows immediately in brackets Rājendralāla Mitra's telling. Also, if the interpretation differs in the shorter stories (as in the *JBTRS* translation) or supports one over the other of the above two interpretations or gives details otherwise left out that are considered important, that interpretation is given last. Note that in the *JBTRS* translation, names are often given incorrectly. When this is the case, these are not always noted. I have referred to the text for the forms of names.

Ten Sufferings. Lord Buddha, during his sojourn by the side of Lake Anavatapta, while giving an account of the former lives of Śāriputra and Maudgalyāyana, illustrated the maxim that "every creature must suffer from the effects of his works" by recounting the ten mundane pains which he suffered. [... This prehistory the Lord narrated in connection with solving a dispute between Śāriputra and Maudgalyāyana who were really the sages Likhita and Saṅkha in their former births. *JBTRS*: Story given at length.] He said:

(1) "In one of my previous existences, when I had the name Kharvota, I killed my half-brother at the instigation of my wife, Kālikā: I have an ulcer on the top of my right toe as a consequence. [Jayanti Chattopadhyay: name = Kharvaṭa. *JBTRS*:

---

this retelling being based on the Buddhist Sanskrit text, in Jayanti Chattopadhyay, 1994, 170–72.

186. *CPD*, vol. 1, p. 234a.

187. *AS*, p. 22, p. 205, and in notes on p. 209 (n. 1), p. 222 (n. 1), p. 228 (n. 10), p. 234 (n. 10), p. 244 (n.1), p. 245 (n. 1, 3, 4), p. 246 (n. 5), p. 247 (n. 1, 2, 3).

188. Verses 138 and 139 were given in *AS* on p. 236 (bottom), and verses 58, 59, and 60 were given on p. 241 (bottom).

Sarvata; text, Kharvvaṭa. Name of place where this occurred, *JBTRS*: Karpata; text, Karpaṭa.]

(2) "As Arthadatta, a merchant, I killed one of my own calling, who was much opposed to my interests. The consequence is, that I have suffered from a sore caused by the prick of a catechu thorn. [When born as the merchant, Arthadatta, he suddenly killed a fellow merchant and as a result, the injury in his toe was not healing. *JBTRS*: A merchant named Arthadatta came with a favouring breeze from Ratnadvīpa with his ship filled with merchandise. Another merchant who had lost his wealth, and had taken shelter with him, attempted secretly to scuttle the ship out of envy. ...]

(3) "In another existence, as Chapala, I threw away, with my own hand, the contents of Upārishya's alms-bowl. This Upārishya was a Pratyeka Buddha. As a result of this outrageous conduct my alms bowl is always empty. [Jayanti Chattopadhyay: ... and as a result had sometimes to return in empty bowl without getting any alms. *JBTRS*: Chapalaka; text, Capalaka. Uparishta; text, Upāriṣṭa.]

(4) "As Bharadvāja, I falsely charged my elder brother Vaśishṭha with holding criminal intercourse with a maid-servant, who was an anchorite; and that is why Sundarī has published a similar scandal against me in my present existence. [Born as Bharadvāja, brother of the sage Vasiṣṭha an Arhat, he did the mischief of spreading the calumny of moral turpitude against him. As a result of the remnant of that sin he had to face accusation by a good looking female mendicant.]

(5) "As a Vaiśya, Mriṇāla by name, I wanted to live with Badrā, a public prostitute, on the condition that she should not allow any body else to have connection with her. Finding her one day in the company of another, in a fit of anger, I killed her. Consequently a Bhikshuṇī has brought a false charge against me in this life. [Then born as Mṛṇāla – he killed one harlot named Bhadrā who, although received remuneration for harlotry from him, double-crossed him and enjoyed the company of another. When the maid of Bhadrā raised hue and cry against Mṛṇāla he escaped with the blood stained weapon and left it in the

hermitage of a Pratyeka Buddha named Suruci. The sentries got the weapon as proof of a crime and apprehended the innocent Pratyeka Buddha. When the innocent saint was about to be executed Mṛṇāla repentantly surrendered and got the release of the Pratyeka Buddha and punishment for his crime. Passing several years in hell as atonement—he yet had to face calumny from a whore.]

(6) "As Manthara, a Brāhmaṇa, finding one day my neighbours giving a splendid feast to Vipaśyī, I railed at them, saying, 'these stupid bald-heads should be fed with barley and weavelled kodra; they do not deserve rich viands.' I have now to live upon kodra and barley in consequence of these irreverent words. [Again born as Māṭhara a brahmin in the Bandhumati city he instigated the people against giving alms to Buddhist Bhikshu like Lord Vipaśyin. As a result he had to eat barley and other inferior quality grains. *JBTRS*: Mathara; text, Maṭhara.]

(7) "Born in ancient days as Uttara, I spoke ill of one Pudgala. I have suffered greatly for it, and had to lead a vicious life for six years in the present existence. [Born as Uttara - he criticized Pudgala (a substance like dvyaṇuka - a diad or a molecule of two atoms according to the Buddhists) and therefore had to perform austere penance for six years. *JBTRS*: As I tarnished the reputation of one Puṅgala, ...; text, Puṅgala.]

(8) "There was a rich patriarch, Dhanavān by name, in the country called Karpaṭa. He had a son named Śrīmān. Tiktamukha, 'bitter-faced,' a medical practitioner of the place, cured Śrīmān of various diseases, but obtained nothing in return. When Śrīmān fell ill again, Tiktamukha put a period to his life by administering a strong poison to him. I was that medical man, and for my treacherous conduct to Śrīmān, I suffer from spermatorrhea in this life. [Jayanti Chattopadhyay: ... As a result he got attacked with diarrhoea. *JBTRS*: ... yet even now I suffer from dysentery.]

(9) "In another existence, as a fisherman, I took great delight at the sight of a large fish under convulsions of death from repeated strokes of the axe. I suffer from cephalgia in

consequence of that demoniacal conduct. [Born as a fisherman's son he readily enjoyed the catching and cutting of two big fishes and consequently he was down with headache when the Śākya clan was facing destruction. *JBTRS*: Two huge fish were formerly dragged out from the water by two fishermen. The fish were cut into pieces. A *Kaivarta* boy who was standing by was delighted at this spectacle. ...]

(10) "Born as an athlete, I treacherously put one of my antagonists to death. I suffer from rheumatism for that deadly sin." [Born as a wrestler – in a competition he unduly brought down a challenger and broke his back and consequently he had still then to suffer from excruciating pain in his back. *JBTRS*: Formerly a certain athletic resident of a village by some artifice, killed a warrior named Bala, in fight. He tore his back in two. ...]

The account of Giuseppe Tucci from Tibetan text follows:

The Ten Sins (Dasakarmapluti). Once some women, prompted by the heretics' wicked advice, tried to tempt the Buddha and for this sin they were damned to Hell. Then, near Lake Anavatapta, Śākyamuni spoke to the assembled monks about the karma he had accumulated in his past lives, whose last consequences he was bearing in his present life. He then sent Maudgalyāyana to call Śāriputra, who was at that moment on Mount Gṛdhrakūṭa, busy sewing his monk's tunic; the two monks vied with each other displaying their magic powers; Śāriputra won the contest, and the Buddha told the story of his past. Once upon a time there were two ascetics, who quarrelled for some trifling reason, and became so furious that one of them called Śaṅkha (*Duṅ*) kicked the other, Likhita (*Bris pa*); the latter then laid this curse upon his comrade: his head, at sunrise, would be blown to pieces. Śaṅkha then stopped the sun's course. Finally Likhita repented and made a clay image of Śaṅkha's head; when the sun rose, the clay head crumbled into fragments and the curse came to an end. Śaṅkha was then Maudgalyāyana and Likhita was Śāriputra.

But, owing to the ripening of his karma, the Buddha too, in his last life upon earth, had undergone various misfortunes.

1) His thumb was crushed by a stone, 2) his foot was pierced by a *khadira* thorn, 3) having gone begging, he had obtained nothing, 4) he had been slandered by women, 5) he had been insulted by some young Brahmans, 6) he had eaten rotten wheat (*kodrava*), 7) during seven seasons he endured penances, 8) he was taken ill, 9) his head ached when the Śākya clan was destroyed, 10) his body suffered fatigue.

"The ties of his karma are to a man like servants ready for a journey, who follow him when he is in motion, and stop in front of him when he stops" (31).

1st Story — Once a rich man called Kharvaṭa (*K'ar ba ṭa*) had in his house a step-brother called Mugdha (*Mug dha*). A woman friend of his named Kālikā (*Nag mo*) repeatedly urged him to kill Mugdha and thus receive the entire family inheritance for himself. At first Kharvaṭa refused, thinking:

"It is not reasonable that people attached to riches should harbour sinful thoughts with the object of (getting) those treasures; all property, even when well guarded, is lost in a moment" (44).

At last, pressed by his friend, he gave in and finally committed the crime. This man was an ancient incarnation of the Buddha; after having atoned for his sin in Hell, in his last incarnation he had wounded his thumb on that account.

2nd Story — Arthadatta (*Don byin*) was coming back from Ratnadvīpa loaded with riches; one of his comrades, who had lost everything, through envy tried to bore a hole in the ship in order to sink it. Arthadatta, unable to turn him from his purpose, finally slew him. Arthadatta was the Buddha; for this act he committed his foot was wounded by a thorn.

3rd Story — When the Pratyekabuddha Upāriṣṭa (*Uparima*, in the prose text: *U pa rin*) came to Kāśi to beg, Capalaka (*gYo ldan*) upset his bowl; Capalaka was the Buddha; for this reason the Buddha's bowl had not been filled.

4th Story — Vasiṣṭha (*Ba si ṣṭha*) and Bharadvāja (*Bha ra dvā dsa*) were brothers; the former being honoured by all as a saint, his brother, envying his fame, borrowed his clothes and gave them to a harlot, in order that she might accuse

Vasiṣṭha of having made her a present of them in exchange for her favours. Bharadvāja was then the Buddha, and through the ripening of that karma, he had been insulted in his present life.

5th Story — In Benares a certain Mṛṇāla (*Pad mai rtsa*, in prose *P. rtsa lag*) loved the courtesan Bhadrā (*bZaṅ mo*) and to reward her services he gave her clothes and jewels. Another suitor appeared and Bhadrā, after long hesitation, listened to the advice of her handmaid Makarikā (*C'u srin ma*) and gave herself to the newcomer. Makarikā disclosed everything to Mṛṇāla who, blinded with jealousy, killed the courtesan. Then, fearing punishment, he fled into the forest and placed the gory dagger near a Pratyekabuddha, but no sooner had the latter been arrested and brought before the judge, that he confessed his sin; owing to a remainder of this evil deed, which he had long atoned for in Hell, the Buddha had now been slandered by heretical women.

6th Story — While the Buddha Vipaśyin was received with great festivities in Bandhumatī (*gÑen ldan*) the Brahman Māṭhara (*Mā ṭha ra*) tried to dissuade the people from honouring him. Māṭhara was then the Buddha who, for his sin, had to eat rotten wheat in this life.

7th Story — In another life Śākyamuni had been Uttara (*Ut ta ra*), who insulted the Buddha of those times; for that sin he now had to do penance for six years before attaining enlightenment.

8th Story — Once a rich lord named Dhanavān (*Nor ldan*) had a son Śrīmān (*dPal ldan*) who was always sickly; the physician Tiktamukha (*K'a bai bžin*) healed him by an appropriate cure, but received no reward from the boy's miserly father; as the case was often repeated, the physician finally poisoned his patient, who died. The physician was the Buddha who, through a remnant of that crime, was subject to illness in this life.

9th Story — When the Buddha was a fisherman's son, he was delighted to see that two fishes had been caught in the net; for this sin he was punished in this life by a headache.

10th Story — In one of his past lives, the Buddha had been a Malla prince who killed his rival and cut him in two; because of a remnant of this crime, he was affected with a disorder of the wind humour.

The Relationship Between the Different Versions of the Text

A few comparisons between the stories as in the different versions are perhaps in order. I restrict myself to comments regarding the Pāli text in *Pkp*, the Sinhalese texts of *UP* and *BN*, the Hīnayāna Sanskrit text as indicated in the Gilgit and Turfan manuscripts and the translations of this as in Tibetan and Chinese versions as translated into German in *AS*, and the Mahāyāna Sanskrit text as in the *Av-klp* of Kṣemendra and its Tibetan translation as retold by Giuseppe Tucci. When considering this last text, I refer generally in the following to the translation from Sanskrit as given in *JBTRS* since this is fuller than the retellings. In one instance I also consider a parallel story in another environment as retold by Nalinaksha Dutt, and in another instance I consider a parallel story as in the *Mahāvastu* as translated by J. J. Jones.[189]

First, though, some general comments are in order.

There is evidence in both the Southern and Northern Buddhist traditions of rounding off the number of stories. The edited Pāli text as presented in *Ap* contains twelve *kamma*s in thirty-two verses, not counting the verse containing the final summation.[190] The Sinhalese texts of *UP* and *BN*, while they present seventeen and twenty-two *kamma*s respectively, refer to themselves as presenting thirty-two *kammas*. The significance of this number was referred to above immediately before the presentation of the Sinhalese text. In the context of the Sinhalese material, it would seem that there was an effort in the Pāli *Apadāna* tradition to achieve a text of thirty-two

189. Nalinaksha Dutt, 1947, pp. 4–5; J. J. Jones, 1949–56, vol. 1, pp. 29-39.
190. *Ap*, pp. 299-301.

verses. The Northern Buddhist versions, while there are at times differences in the stories recounted and in the ordering of the stories, all present ten *kammas*.

In the specific case of the *Av-klp*, while the chapter in question refers to itself as presenting ten *kamma*s and while the various retellings only note ten *kammas*, verse 71 of the text reflected in the full translation in *JBTRS* presents the first part of still another *kamma*.[191] This is reference to a third "slandering" story, corresponding to the third "slandering" story in the Pāli text of the *Pkp* that resulted in the Buddha's last lifetime in slander of the 500 monks because of Sundarīkā. Kṣemendra's text otherwise refers only to two "slanderings", unlike the other Northern Buddhist versions, which refer to all three.

In the specific case of the Turfan manuscript reported by *AS* there is also evidence of an eleventh *kamma*. This corresponds to one of the stories represented in the material here only in the *Av-klp*, placed there as the third *kamma*.[192] *AS* lists this as its *kamma* no. 10a. It is not clear whether another of the *kamma*s was omitted in the Sanskrit text of the *Anavataptagāthā* as in the Turfan manuscripts, since the text here has not been preserved except for very few passages.

Earlier when first presenting the additional initial *kamma* found in Thai manuscripts of the *Pkp* and in the Sinhalese texts of *UP* and *BN*, I expressed the opinion that this passage was original in the Pali tradition of the *Pkp*. I also believe it to be original in the overall textual tradition of the text, but to have been omitted in the Northern Buddhist texts of which we have evidence. When we take into consideration that both the Southern and Northern Budddhist traditions have rounded off the number of *kamma*s presented, and add to this consideration the perhaps offending nature from the vantage of Buddhism of this *kamma*, and the consideration that this *kamma* frames all that follows, we are led to this conclusion. What is offending

191. See *JBTRS* 1.4 (1893), on p. 22.

192. See *AS*, p. 241. *AS*, p. 241, n.3 refers to a few other places where this *kamma* is mentioned.

about this *kamma* is that it implies that the Buddha, albeit in a former life, had craving or thirst. This, of course, is what ties one to rebirth.[193] It is unlikely that such a passage would be added in the tradition. Note the opinion of S. M. Cutler that the versions of the *Apadāna* that are available to us now reveal we possess a corrupt and late redaction of the text.[194] Also note that the following verse in the Pāli text refers to *pubbe aññāsu jātisu*, "in a past life, among other lives". As noted above, this suggests that the verse in question is a continuation. Note that no other Pāli verse in this text begins with this locution.

It is more difficult to decide whether the two *kammas* involving Devadatta that are not included in the Northern Buddhist tradition are original to the textual tradition, or are additions in the Theravada tradition. As noted above, when presenting the outline in chart form of *BN* and *UP*, the *Pkp* is perfectly balanced. Three stories involving the Buddha's troubles with unvirtuous women are followed by three stories involving the Buddha's troubles with an unvirtuous man, Devadatta. Then there follow two sequences of three stories each involving sickness, personal harm (and perhaps sickness as well), and difficulty in religion. This sequence is upset in the Northern Buddhist versions of the text.

It is compensated for, though, by a de-emphasis of the person of Devadatta in the *kamma* involving Devadatta which is included, such that the *Av-klp* does not even mention him. It focuses, instead, on the wounding of the Buddha's toe with a sharp flint (introduction), or on the sore on the Buddha's toe (narration). This de-emphasis of the person of Devadatta is also achieved through an emphasis on the act of murder by the Buddha in his past lives. The *kamma* which follows the story involving Devadatta which the Northern Buddhist tradition includes, in the Pāli tradition involves striking a man with a dagger while previously an earthly king, in the Sinhalese tradition stabbing a man at the order of a king while in the

193. See the discussion in *PED*, p. 294ab under Pāli *taṇha* "thirst; fig. craving".
194. S. M. Cutler, 1994, pp. 36–37.

king's service. The Northern Buddhist tradition, though, has here a story of a merchant onboard a ship who kills a fellow merchant with a dagger, knife, or spear-point depending on the version. *AS* characterizes these two incidents as "Murder with a Rock" and "Murder with a Dagger", and would see the latter as a variation of the Pāli story. Nalinaksha Dutt sees the two stories as being different.[195] The Pāli variant reading *satthako*, "caravan merchant", or "belonging to a caravan" for *patthivo* in the *Pkp* perhaps suggests a possible connection between the Southern and Northern Buddhist stories here.

The story that follows these two involves a fisherboy's "Delight at the Killing of Fish". In all these three *kammas*, it is physical ailments in the Buddha's present life that are emphasized and can be seen as a common element to these stories, though the story of "Murder with a Dagger" as in *Taishō* no. 199 mentions only subsequent life in hell, and as in *Taishō* no. 197 mentions only subsequent lives in hell, as an animal, and as a *preta*—the last two of which are not mentioned elsewhere.[196]

Also leading to physical ailments in the two traditions are the *kammas* involving the Buddha having been in former lives a doctor and a Malla. In the Northern Buddhist tradition the patient is murdered in the first story, as in *Taishō* no. 197 and in *Av-klp*. This is not so in the Tibetan text and in *Taishō* no. 199. The Malla opponent is, according to the Northern Buddhist tradition, killed in the other story. This is not so in either case in the Pāli text of *Pkp* or in the Sinhalese tradition of *UP* and *BN*. In the story about Mṛṇāla in the *Av-klp*, the murder of a courtesan by Mṛṇāla is introduced. This is not mentioned earlier, though both Chinese versions of the story mention that the *pratyekabuddha* slandered by Mṛṇāla had been sentenced to death. In the *Av-klp* account Mṛṇāla places the bloodstained weapon in the sage's hermitage, and he is falsely accused of the murder.

---

195. See Nalinaksha Dutt, 1947, p. 25 for the lacuna. Dutt gives Tibetan text only for passages he sees as corresponding in the Pāli and Tibetan text.
196. See *AS*, p. 227.

All this does not lead, however, to a balanced organization as in the Pāli *Pkp*. The *Av-klp* perhaps attempts to achieve better organization in its ordering of the stories, emphasizing the focus on murder organizationally as well, but it does not quite achieve this. This ordering, interestingly, is similar to the ordering in a prose retelling of the text in the Gilgit manuscripts that, however, is missing leaves at its beginning and end. Because of this, we cannot be entirely sure if the entire ordering of *kammas* was the same.

Given what would appear to be an instability in the ordering of the *kammas* in the Northern Buddhist tradition, the lack of a balanced organization of the *kammas* in the Pāli *Pkp* and in the Sinhalese texts in *UP* and *BN*, and the seeming attempt to compensate for this by introducing variant stories and shifting emphasis to an act of murder, I would judge that the Devadatta cycle of three stories as in the Pāli *Pkp* is original in our textual tradition.

The Organization of the Text in the Northern Buddhist Versions

So that the reader can see more clearly what I am referring to regarding the organization of the text in the Northern Buddhist versions, I give here a charting of the text as in the *Anavataptagāthā* as presented by *AS*, as in the *Av-klp*, and as in the incomplete prose summary in the Gilgit manuscripts as presented by Nalinaksha Dutt. Both on the basis of the organization of the text, and on the basis of textual parallels that will be brought out below, such as parallels in the telling of the two stories of slander that are given fully in the *Av-klp*, we can judge that *Av-klp* 50 and the Gilgit manuscripts' prose retelling of the text constitute a Kashmiri recension of the text. In the charting, I use both *AS*'s characterizations of the stories, which focus on the antecedent action, and characterizations of the stories in line with my outline for *BN* and *UP* above which focus on the consequent *kammas*. At times, I add to *AS*'s characterizations of the antecedent actions further characterizations or clarifications so as to add further clarity to the outline. These are placed in square brackets. In the *Av-klp* the ordering of the stories is the same in both the introduction to the narration and in the narration proper. The only differences are that the narration proper includes one verse making reference to what in the Pali *Pkp* is a third "slandering", and that the introduction makes reference to Cañcā[197] who is not referred to by name in the narration of the relevant story.

Anavataptagatha[198]

I. The first slandering. / Trouble with unvirtuous women.
II. The second slandering. [The third slandering in *Pkp*, *BN*, and *UP*.] / Trouble with unvirtuous women.
III. The third slandering. [The second slandering in *Pkp*, *BN*, and *UP*.] / Trouble with unvirtuous women.
IV. Murder with a rock. / [Devadatta.] Physical ailment.
V. Murder with a dagger [at sea]. / Physical ailment [Tibetan text].
VI. Delight at the killing of fish. / Physical ailment.
VII. Eating barley. [Ill-considered speech.] / Difficulty in religion (alms).
VIII. The sinful doctor. [Murder, *Taishō* no. 197.] / Physical ailment.
IX. Knocking down a Malla. [Murder.] / Physical ailment.
X. Slandering the Buddha Kāśyapa. [Ill-considered speech.] / Difficulty in religion (obtaining enlightenment).
Xa. [Upsetting the alms bowl of the Pratyeka Buddha Upāriṣṭa (incomplete reference to in three partially preserved verses only).] / Difficulty in religion (alms).

The Kashmiri Recension

A. *Bodhisattvāvadānakalpalatā* (*Av-klp*), Chapter 50

I. Murder with a rock. / Physical ailment.

---

197. Cañcā = Pāli Ciñca, regarding which see below.
198. *AS*, pp. 208–48.

II. Murder with a dagger [at sea]. / Physical ailment.
III. [Upsetting the alms bowl of the Pratyeka Buddha Upāriṣṭa.] / Difficulty in religion (alms).
IV. The third slandering [variation]. / Trouble with unvirtuous women.
IVa. The second slandering (incomplete reference to in one verse only).
V. The first slandering [and murder]. / Trouble with unvirtuous women.
VI. Eating barley. [Ill-considered speech.] / Difficulty in religion, 3 months duration (alms).
VII. [Slandering. Perhaps just ill-considered speech according to one interpretation.] / Difficulty in religion, 6 years duration (obtaining enlightenment, alms).
VIII. The sinful doctor. [Murder.] / Physical ailment.
IX. Delight at the killing of fish. / Physical ailment.
X. Knocking down a Malla. [Murder.] / Physical ailment.

B. Gilgit Manuscripts' Incomplete Prose Retelling[199]

[Leaves missing.]
III. The third slandering [variation].
IV. The second slandering.
V. The first slandering [and murder]. / Trouble with unvirtuous women.
VI. Eating barley. [Ill-considered speech.] / Difficulty in religion, 3 months duration (alms).
VII. Slandering the Buddha Kāśyapa. [Ill-considered speech.] / Difficulty in religion, 6 years duration (obtaining enlightenment).
VIII. The sinful doctor. [Murder.] / Physical ailment.
[Leaves missing.]

---

199. Nalinaksha Dutt, 1947, pp. 28–29.

Further Nature of the Tradition: Textual Tradition versus Oral Tradition

To be emphasized is that we clearly have here a textual tradition, not just an oral tradition. This is indicated by the close correspondence between the Pāli *Pkp* and the corresponding Tibetan text, as pointed out for instance by Nalinaksha Dutt and by *AS*.[200] In most instances, there is a one-to-one correspondence between the verses of the Pāli *Pkp* and the Tibetan verses, albeit each text has verses or passages that the other does not have. Especially to be noted is that we have occasional transposition of sections of verses, as pointed out by *AS*.[201] Thus, *Pkp* verse 8cd (*Pkp* story 2 on Ciñca, or Ciñcī) appears following *Pkp* verse 5ab as Tibetan verse 685cd (*Pkp* story 1 on Munāli), and *Pkp* verse 5d (*Pkp* story 1 on Munāli) appears following *Pkp* verse 8ab as Tibetan verse 693d (*Pkp*, story 2 on Ciñcī).

AS comments that in general the Tibetan text and the Chinese text as in *Taishō* no. 199 are similar to one another. But in some instances, the Tibetan text is more similar to the Chinese text of *Taishō* no. 197.[202] Thus, in the story of the slandering of the Buddha Kāśyapa, there is no doubt that the name of the slanderer is Nandipāla (or Jotipāla in the Pali *Pkp* and the Sinhalese *BN* and *UP*). However, in both the Tibetan text and in *Taishō* no. 197 Nandipāla is not the name of the slanderer (as in *Taishō* no. 199), but the name of the man to whom the slander is spoken, while the slanderer takes another name. The name of the slandered Buddha Kāśyapa (P. Kassapa) is mentioned only in the Pāli *Pkp*, Sinhalese *BN* and *UP*, and in *Taishō* no. 199. Also regarding the word *āgataṃ* in *Pkp* verse 11, *AS* notes the remarkable agreement between the Pāli text here and the Chinese text in *Taishō* no. 199, while the Tibetan text stands nearer to the Chinese text in *Taishō* no. 197.[203]

---

200. Nalinaksha Dutt, 1947, pp. 21–28; *AS*, pp. 208–48.
201. *AS*, p. 212 and p. 214.
202. *AS*, p. 239, n. 2.
203. *AS*, p. 215, n. 6.

Perhaps we have a textual tradition supplemented by an oral tradition, or at the very least auxiliary stories that are being drawn from. As in the case of the story of the slander by the Bodhisatta of a disciple of the Buddha Sarvābhibhū (P. Sabbābhibhū) in the Mahāsaṅghika *Mahāvastu-avadāna*, or the story of the Buddha having had to eat barley for three months in Verajjā and its karmic cause recounted in the Gilgit manuscripts in a section prior to the *Sthaviragāthā*.[204]

Some of the stories, however, appear to undergo changes in the course of their transmission, much as something whispered from one person to another becomes transformed. The varying references to Nandipāla, or Jotipāla, as the slanderer of the Buddha Kāśyapa (P. Kassapa) on the one hand, and as the person to whom the slander is spoken on the other hand is an example of this. Further, in the story of the slander by the Bodhisatta of a disciple of the Buddha Sarvābhibhū (P. Sabbābhibhū), which leads in the Buddha's last life to his slander by Ciñcī, *Pkp* mentions the name of the disciple, Nanda, and the name of the Buddha only. *BN* and *UP* also mention Nanda as the name of the disciple who was slandered, but they refer to Sabbābhibhū as Vessabhū. The corresponding Tibetan text, on the other hand, names the slandered disciple of Sarvābhibhū as Vasiṣṭha. Similarly, *Taishō* no. 199 mentions a disciple Chi-shih-cha (= Ho-shih-cha, or Vasiṣṭha)[205] of the Buddha I-ch'ieh-ming (Sarvavidū),[206] who was slandered. *Taishō* no. 197 names the slandering monk as To-huan (Nanda), and refers to the Buddha of whom he was a disciple as Chin-chêng (*i.e.* Śāntiyeṣṭha ?). The Mahāsaṅghika *Mahāvastu-avadāna*, in the passage cited above, would on the other hand have the slandered monk to be named Nanda, as in the Pāli and Sinhalese traditions, and would have the slandering monk's name to be Abhiya. Both were followers of the Buddha Sarvābhibhū. The account of the *Av-klp* omits reference to a Buddha of whom the two are disciples, and would have the

204. For the former, see J. J. Jones, 1949–56, vol. 1, pp. 29–39. For the latter, see Nalinaksha Dutt, 1947, pp. 4–5.
205. See *AS*, p. 219, n. 5.
206. See *AS*, p. 219, n. 3.

slanderer and the slandered be brothers. The slandered brother is an *arhant* named Vaśiṣṭha living in a *vihāra* consecrated by the citizens for his use. The slanderer was his jealous younger brother, a *pravrajaka* (ascetic), named Bharadvāja. Showing again the close relationship between the prose retelling in the Gilgit manuscripts and the *Av-klp*, and suggesting that the *Av-klp* is drawing on comparable text, the prose retelling in the Gilgit manuscripts here also refers to two brothers, Vaśiṣṭha and Bharadvāja, except here Bharadvāja is the elder brother and Vasiṣṭha the younger. "Bharadvāja was looked after by a devoted householder. He invited his brother Vasiṣṭha to stay with him. The latter made such a good impression on the householder that he received more gifts than his elder brother. This roused the envy of Bharadvāja, who made the maid servant of the house throw calumny on his brother and thereby brought discredit on him."[207] The transformations here are significant, and would seem to indicate oral transmission because of this.

Thus also, in the story of the sinful physician, *Pkp* states only that the physician purged the son of a wealthy merchant. The Tibetan text states that the physician gave the son of a wealthy merchant an incurable case of diarrhea. But the Sinhalese texts of *BN* and *UP* note further that the physician noticed that the merchant was not going to pay, and so gave the patient (in this case, the merchant himself) incompatible medicine. Similarly, the Sanskrit prose retelling in the Gilgit manuscripts notes that he cured a householder's son twice, but did not get paid. When the patient took ill a third time, the physician gave him such a medicine that his intestines were destroyed. And similarly, in the *Av-klp*, the physician named here Titktamukha (so text, as well as retellings) treats a number of times the son, named Śrīmān, of the householder Dhanavān. He does not get paid. So the physician becomes angry and when the son takes ill again, he prescribes a drug that would dry up his intestines. It would seem that we have here a tradition on which the Sinhalese texts of *BN* and *UP*, the Sanskrit retelling in the Gilgit manuscripts,

---

207. Nalinaksha Dutt, 1947, pp. 28–29.

and the *Av-klp* are drawing, but which is not hinted at in the Pāli text of *Pkp* or the corresponding Tibetan text. In the Chinese versions, it is only *Taishō* no. 197 that hints at the situation described above. It notes that the physician treated the son of a merchant, and that out of anger gave the patient incorrect medicine, causing him to die. *Taishō* no. 199 notes only that the physician treated the son of a merchant, and incorrectly put together the components of his medicine, such that the patient's sickness took a turn for the worse.

Similarly, in the story of knocking down a Malla, *Pkp* noted only that the Buddha in his earlier existence restrained a Mallaputta in a wrestling competition (*Ap S*: injured a Mallaputta). The Tibetan text notes that in his former existence he was a powerful fist-fighter, and that he killed a fist-fighter in athletic competition. The Pāli word used for the wrestling competition, would also allow itself to be understood as a fist-fighting competition. And a Malla might perhaps just as well be understood as a fist-fighter as well as a wrestler. But usage of the verb *nisedhayiṃ* "restrained" in *Pkp* suggests a wrestling competition. Compare, though, *Ap S*. In *BN* and *UP* the Buddha in his former existence was born in a Mallava (wrestler) family. He pinched down another wrestler, and wrung his back. The focus here clearly is on the competition being a wrestling competition. The prose retelling as in the Gilgit manuscripts is missing for this story. But the *Av-klp* would have the Buddha have been in his former existence an athlete who killed a warrior named Bala in a fight, tearing his back in two. In the Chinese texts, *Taishō* no. 197 similarly notes that the Buddha in his previous existence, at a fighting competition, with a blow struck his opponent to the ground such that his back broke right through the middle. Taisho no. 199, on the other hand, notes only that the Buddha in his previous existence was a fist-fighter who, fighting with a Malla named Yo-fu-tzŭ injured and killed him.[208] Clearly, here again we have an ancillary tradition that is reflected in the Sinhalese

208. *AS*, p. 237, n. 1 explains the Malla's name Yo-fu-tzŭ as being a literary expansion. See the note regarding the specifics of this.

BN and *UP*, the Sanskrit *Av-klp*, and in the Chinese version in Taisho no. 197. The difference, on the other hand, between the Southern texts referring alternately to the athletic competition as a wrestling competition, or the Buddha or his opponent as wrestlers, and the Northern Buddhist tradition referring to a fist-fighting competition, or referring to the two as being fist-fighters, has the appearance of being due to a difference in a reading in the two traditions, perhaps in the verb that appears in the Pāli text as in *Ap*, as noted within this paragraph.

Just as the *Av-klp* inserts proverbs and proverbial wisdom, the Chinese text in *Taishō* 197 inserts several verses of sermonizing at the end of every story. The verses in question are repeated almost formulaically, though occasionally some of the verses are alternated so as not to give the impression of too rigid a structure. The force and formulaic nature of the sermonizing, though, remains. This is perhaps comparable to the formulaic refrain at the end of every *kamma* narrated in the Sinhalese text of *BN*, and perhaps to some extent in *UP*, which states, "This, O monks, is one *karma*," or "O monks, this is another *karma*." This, though, is less an aspect of the tradition as such, than of common stylistic practices shared in the larger tradition.

What is part of our textual tradition proper is the inclusion in the Tibetan text, and in the two Chinese versions of our text, of a verse stating that the Buddha spent time in hell, or hells, for his evil deed, in almost all the stories. This is placed after the narration of the antecedent action, and before the narration of the subsequent *kamma* in this last life as Buddha. It is only the first two stories in the Pāli *Pkp* and in the corresponding stories in the Sinhalese *BN* and *UP* which similarly have the Bodhisatta spending lengthy periods of time in hell. It is on the basis of such a verse appearing in almost every story in the Tibetan text, but not in the Pāli *Pkp*, that led Nalinaksha Dutt to conclude that the two texts were derived from a common third source.[209] To be considered in this regard, though, is that our standard text of the *Pkp* may have eliminated such verses in its

---

209. Nalinaksha Dutt, 1947, p. 28.

attempt to achieve a text of 32 verses, not counting the verse containing the final summation.

Local traditions and local color are also inserted into the textual tradition here.

In the story of the slander by the Bodhisatta of a disciple of the Buddha Sarvābhibhū (P. Sabbābhibhū), the Chinese text in *Taishō* no. 199 refers to the hell T'ai-shan. This indicates Taoist belief. This is a hell located under the tree T'ai in the province of Shantung. *AS* comments that the popular ideas of the hereafter of the Chinese mix Buddhist and Taoist thought.[210] This hell is also mentioned in this translation, along with the *Kālasūtra* hell, in the following story of murder with a rock. And the two hells are mentioned in this translation in the story about eating barley. *AS* indicates that the Chinese had two different hells, and that this matches the Tibetan text's mentioning the *Pratāpana* and the *Kālasūtra* hells. But the translator understood *pratāpana* as an attribute of *kālasūtra* and in free fashion translated it as a verb.[211]

The story about delight at the killing of fish also introduces local color. In the Sinhalese texts of *BN* and *UP*, the catching of the fish with nets is introduced, as is putting the fish caught in a heap. This suggests fishing practices prevalent in Sri Lanka and parts of India. In the Chinese text of *Taishō* no. 197, the caught fish are laid down on the shore and hit with a stick on the head. In the *Av-klp*, two large fish are dragged out from the water, and then cut into pieces. According to Giuseppe Tucci's interpretation of the Tibetan translation of this text, the two fish were caught in a net. In the Pāli *Pkp* and in the corresponding Tibetan text, it is only mentioned that fish were killed, and in the Chinese text of *Taishō* no. 199 it is stated only that fish were caught and killed.

The Sinhalese texts of *BN* and *UP* are especially noteworthy for introducing local color. In the story regarding the eating of barley, rice made of local *äl* paddy is mentioned as being good

---

210. *AS*, p. 221, n. 1.

211. *AS*, p. 223, n. 3. See Bechert's note for further specifics.

enough for the teasing monk. In the story of knocking down a Malla, the Buddha is mentioned to have the strength of 10 crores (i.e., millions) of elephants of the *kālava* species, which species of elephant has the strength of ten men. A reference such as this would probably be lost on a Tibetan or Chinese person, who would not be knowledgeable of elephants and elephant lore.

In general, there appear to be differences in the way in which the tradition is expanded in the Southern Buddhist texts and the Northern Buddhist texts being considered here. As noticed above, there is evidence that initially in both traditions, from the vantage of the texts available to us, there was contraction of the tradition.

In the Sinhalese tradition represented by *BN* and *UP*, the tradition was expanded by adding stories in a balanced fashion that was consonant with the existing structure of the Pāli *Pkp*. In the case of *UP*, since there were no additional stories of antecedent actions to relate to the additional instances of misfortune being noted, these were not included. In the case of *BN*, in the stories it receives from *UP* which it presents, this is also the case. It substitutes a different story only with regard to the *kamma* involving schism. In the additional stories that *BN* presents, however, antecedent actions were taken from the *Jātakas*, and these are matched *UP* with incidents from the Buddha's life. The last *kamma* in *BN* involves things that happened after the Buddha's death to one of his tooth relics. In presenting this, the concluding summation of *UP* is contradicted. This latter states that at the time of the delivery of the sermon in *Pkp* and *UP* the Buddha had exhausted both the beneficial consequences of meritorious deeds and any evil consequences of deeds that might occur in the future. This summation is omitted in *BN*, as is any reference to *Pkp*, verses 31–32, and 33, to which it corresponds. Further, the stories in *UP*, while they are lengthier and perhaps more detailed than those presented in *Pkp*, are nevertheless short. The additional stories added by *BN* are lengthier. They are nevertheless summaries of the stories they are presenting, which are recorded elsewhere in Buddhist literature with only one exception—story XVIIb.

In the Northern Buddhist tradition, once the number of stories had been set at ten, this never changed. Instead, different stories were substituted for others, as would seem to have happened in the instance of the antecedent action in the story of murder with a dagger. Also, this would appear to be the case regarding the story of upsetting the alms bowl of the *pratyekabuddha* Upāriṣṭa. This appears instead of one of the slandering stories in the *Av-klp*, and it seems likely that it too substituted for a story in the missing Sanskrit passages for our text as in the Turfan manuscripts. Also, there are significant differences in the story of the third slandering in the antecedent action as in the *Av-klp* and in the incomplete prose retelling of the Gilgit manuscripts' account. Further, we find in the Northern Buddhist tradition occasional lengthier versions of some of the stories that give additional details and names, as in the case of the story of the slander by the Bodhisatta of a disciple of the Buddha Sarvābhibhū (P. Sabbābhibhū) in the *Mahāvastu-avadāna*, and in the case of some of the stories in Kṣemendra's *Av-klp*. In some instances, the stories in Kṣemendra's text are true variant stories. This suggests that the origins of these stories lie in the Buddhist Sanskrit tradition, as has been previously suggested.

Discussions of Three Specific Stories

A. The First Slandering: The Story of Munāli

The first story treating Munāli (Skt. Mṛṇāla), the fifth story in the *Av-klp*, provides examples of some of the points made here. In the Pāli *Pkp* it mentions simply that Munāli was a scoundrel, and that he slandered an innocent *paccekabuddha* named Surabhi.

BN and *UP*, while not mentioning the name of the *paccekabuddha*, expand on this. They state that Munāli was born in a family of tailors, and that Munāli was the family name. They state that Munāli honored *paccekabuddhas*, but that with a defiled mind he accused a virtuous *paccekabuddha* whom he had seen in the city begging alms of having done and said things that he had not, and having sexual intercourse with women. This develops the story in a way different from what is found in the Northern Buddhist tradition. Though it does have the *paccekabuddha* being accused of having sexual intercourse with women, as would make sense given the subsequent *kamma* in the Buddha's last life, it would appear to be an independent development of the story.

The corresponding Tibetan text names the *pratyekabuddha* Suruci, refers to Mṛṇāla as a swindler or con man, and like the Pāli *Pkp* simply states that Mṛṇāla slandered the faultless *pratyekabuddha*. The Tibetan text, though, includes two additional verses that are not reflected in the *Pkp*. The first states that while the *muni* was in a large assembly of people, he was bound and let out of town. The second states that Mṛṇāla, seeing the ascetic bound and about to suffer misfortune, had compassion toward Suruci and he was therefore set free on account of Mṛṇāla.

The Chinese text in *Taishō* no. 199 refers to the *pratyekabuddha* as Shan-miao, which *AS* comments corresponds to Sundarananda, and here stands for the name Suruci which has a similar meaning.[212] Mṛṇāla, here Wên-lo, is referred to just as a man, but it is stated he reviled the *pratyekabuddha*. A great number of men came together and tied up Shan-miao. The text here amplifies on the Tibetan text, and states that they locked Shan-miao in jail as a prisoner, tied up and condemned to death. Meanwhile Mṛṇāla, having seen the *śramaṇa* being led away bound, developed compassion toward him in his heart, and saw to it that he was freed. *Taishō* no. 197 refers to the *pratyekabuddha* as Lo-wu, refers to Mṛṇāla as the gambler Ching-yen ("Pure-eye"), and states that the *pratyekabuddha*, without himself having done anything wrong, obtained great poverty on account of Ching-yen. Agreeing with *Taishō* no. 199, it states that even though truthful and pure, Lo-wu was attacked by the crowd, and with insult and disgrace was bound up and lead to the place

---

212. *AS*, p. 213, n. 1.

of execution. Seeing the *pratyekabuddha* being bound and humiliated, Ching-yen became overcome with compassion and arranged for his release.

What is left out in these Northern Buddhist stories suggests that the brevity of the account in these few verses, even briefer in *Pkp*, is intentionally done to stir further discussion. It is possible, though, that the additional verses in the Northern Buddhist versions were omitted in *Pkp* specifically to avoid such discussion in this instance, at least. To be kept in mind here, though, is that our present text of *Pkp* shows signs of having been abbreviated so as to create a text of thirty-two verses, not counting the verse containing the final summation.

What is left out here, we find in full detail in the *Av-klp*. To be considered here is that chapter 50 of the *Av-klp* is in total 142 verses long. The narration of the stories proper starts with verse 35, so that the narration of the stories is 108 verses long. The narration of the story regarding Mṛṇāla extends from verses 72–116, being 45 verses in length, or almost half the length of the entire narration proper. Again showing the close relationship between this chapter of the *Av-klp* and the incomplete prose retelling of this text in the Gilgit manuscripts, this retelling gives the same story in briefer format and without all the added proverbs and bits of proverbial wisdom. "Śākyamuni was once born as a wicked man called Mṛṇāla who lived with a courtesan called Bhadrā. On one occasion Mṛṇāla found out that Bhadrā was entertaining another person, so he flew into a rage and killed her outright. There was a great uproar and Mṛṇāla, finding a hermit nearby who was a Pratyekabuddha, left the blood-stained sword near him and joined the crowd, which fixed the guilt on the Pratyekabuddha and brought him before the king. When the hermit was being led to the gallows, Mṛṇāla became repentant and confessed his guilt."[213]

The result of all this in the Buddha's last life was, according to the *Pkp*, that he received slander because of Sundarīkā.

213. Nalinaksha Dutt, 1947, p. 29.

BN and *UP* expand on this in accord with the story as told elsewhere in the Pāli Buddhist canon. They state that in this life the Buddha received a similar accusation to the one he had made in his former life about the *paccekabuddha* (according to *BN* and *UP*). Sundarī told the public that she had been living with the Buddha in a perfumed chamber, and thus disgraced him.

The Tibetan text, also in accord with the Pāli canonical story, states that in the Buddha's last existence he received slanderous rebuke from the heretics because of Sundarī.

The Chinese text of *Taishō* no. 199 agrees with the Tibetan text, stating that because of Hsü-t'o-li (Sundarī) the heretics all talked, falsely blaming the Buddha and slandering him. *Taishō* no. 197 at first states only that in his last existence the Buddha was slandered. But then, after stating that the Buddha has now cut off all rebirth and exhausted his *kamma*, it refers to a different version of the story in which the slanderer of the Buddha herself did the slandering. *AS* compares this to the story of Ciñcī in Pāli texts, in which the Buddha was abused by the approaching slanderer as he was explaining his teachings before a crowd.[214]

AS remarks in passing that Sundarī and Cañcā were often mixed up.[215] The prose account of the second slandering of the Tibetan text of the *Mūlasarvāstivinaya*, in contrast to the Tibetan verses, claim that the slanderer was Cañcā instead of Sundarī. This also explains the transposed sections of verses in the Tibetan text as against the Pāli *Pkp* as a result of textual tradition. The transposed sections of verses are between this story treating Munāli and Sundarī, and the story about Ciñcī. Léon Feer gives the opinion that all these slandering stories are about Ciñca, and that Sundarī, or Sundarikā, is just an epithet or surname.[216]

Showing the confusion as well, the Gilgit manuscripts' prose summary for this story states that the Buddha in his last life was calumniated by Cañcā-māṇavikā. The *Av-klp* states only that the Buddha in his last life, as a result of his earlier deed, was

214. *AS*, p. 215, n. 2.
215. *AS*, p. 244, n. 3.
216. Léon Feer, 1897, p. 293, pp. 296–97.

falsely accused by the *tīrthhika* (heretic) women of having had connection with them. The introduction to this text, though, questions, "Why has the dwarf Banchá falsely accused thee ... [?]" The name Banchá is a Bengali Anglicization for Vañcā, which is how the text here reads. "V" is a common script confusion for "c", and vice versa, in *Devanāgarī* and *Jainanāgarī* scripts. The name of the slanderer is Cañcā in the North and Ciñca in the South.[217] The reference to Cañcā as a dwarf is due to a misunderstanding of *māṇavikā* "a young girl (esp. a young Brahman girl)" as meaning contemptuously, "a little person".[218] Interestingly, the preceding story of slander in the *Av-klp* attributes the false accusation against the Buddha in this last life to have come from Sundarī, and the introduction questions, "... why has the *Prabrájiká* Sundarí falsely aspersed thee [?]" The corresponding story in the incomplete prose summary of the text in the Gilgit manuscripts does not mention the *kamma* in the Buddha's last life.

B. Eating Barley

A second story we might profitably compare the different versions of is that regarding eating barley. The *Pkp* simply states that in a previous life the Buddha reviled disciples of the word of Phussa, saying that they should not eat rice, but rather should eat and munch the inferior barley.

BN and *UP* elaborate this. The Buddha was a layman. A disciple monk of the Buddha Phussa, here in the singular, was learning Pāli texts. Seeing that he had abundant alms, the Buddha teased him saying that given a choice between the good to eat monk's barley and rice made from *äl* paddy, he would *settle* for the rice. In fact, barley grains are the inferior food.

In the Tibetan text, the Buddha in his previous life is made to curse a disciple of the Buddha Vipaśyin, saying that he deserves to eat only barley and that it is not right that he should eat rice. Unlike *Pkp*, but as in *BN* and *UP*, the curse is here directed at a single disciple.

---

217. Léon Feer, 1897, p. 296.
218. See *MW*, p. 806b.

All the Northern Buddhist texts with the single exception of the Chinese text in *Taishō* no. 197, in contrast to the Southern Buddhist texts, refer to Vipaśyin as the Buddha here.

Among the Chinese texts, *Taishō* no. 199, like the Tibetan text, keeps the text short and simple. During the time of the exalted Wei-wei (Vipaśyin),[219] the Buddha in a former life cursed a student of Wei-wei's, again in the singular, saying, "Do not eat rice. Always you should chew red barley." The text then adds, as part of its statement that the Buddha went to the *Kālasūtra* hell for his offence and suffered immeasurable pain, that this was because as a (Brahman) teacher he had uttered bad speech out of his mouth. The Tibetan text in its statement that the Buddha suffered many sorrows in the *Kālasūtra* hell, also states that this was due to nasty speech but it does not mention that the Buddha was a teacher. The text of *Taishō* no. 197 elaborates on this. The Buddha in his earlier existence was a *brahmacārin* whose learning was extensive and thorough. He taught 500 youths in a park. In the time of the Buddha P'i-shê,[220] he formally cursed the *bhikṣu* saying, "You should not eat rice. To be fair, you should eat barley for horses." His youths further declared that the monks of the master also should eat horse barley. The reason for the text introducing the Buddha in his former life here as a Brahman teacher of 500 youths who similarly curse the Buddha P'i-shê's monks is to explain why in the Buddha's last life not only he but also his accompanying 500 monks had to eat barley for the three months of the rainy season retreat spent in Vairambha. It is also an allusion to the 500 monks assembled at Anavatapta Lake to whom this sermon is being preached, and who are treated as equivalent.[221] The text, of course, adds that on account of the bad *kamma* from this deed, both the Buddha and his students suffered the pain of hell for a long time.

---

219. *AS*, p. 223, n. 1 comments that for Wei-wei as a translation of Vipaśyin, see *Taishō* no. 4.

220. *AS*, p. 233, n. 2 mentions that P'i-shê is a transcription for Viśvabhuj according to E. Waldschmidt, *Mahāvadānasūtra*, p. 169. Compare, though, with the name Phussa of *Pkp*, *BN*, and *UP*.

221. See *AS*, p. 223, n. 4.

The narration of the incomplete prose summary of the Gilgit manuscripts is essentially the same as *Taishō* no. 197, except the name of the Buddha involved is Vipaśyin. For this narration, the incomplete prose summary refers to an earlier narration in the Gilgit manuscripts, in a section prior to the *Sthaviragatha*, which describes the Buddha's stay at Vairambha.[222] Dutt states that the story in the two places is the same. In this text the Buddha himself casts aspersions on Vipaśyin and his disciples, saying that they all deserved only barley grains and not the good food offered by the faithful. This here was assented to by 498 students but disapproved by two. As a result of this all of them except for Śāriputra and Maudgalyāyana, who were the two disapproving students, had to live on barley grains in Vairambha.

The narration of the *Av-klp* adds additional names not given before, and eliminates the Brahman's students. In this account, the blessed *jina* Vipaśyin together with his monks and devotees were staying in the city of Bandhumati where the citizens were furnishing them with all articles of enjoyment. The Buddha was at that time a Brahman named Maṭhara. He told the citizens that since the Buddhist mendicants did not have a tuft of hair on the crown of their head, like the Brahmans, they did not deserve to be treated with dainties. The palate of those mendicants who have the crowns of their heads shaven was not for delicious food. They ought to have been served with the old *kodrava* (*Paspalum scrobiculatum*) grain. Thus, the *JBTRS* translation. The text, though, mentions both *kodrava* and barley in both the text proper and the introduction. So also do the interpretations of this Sanskrit passage other than that of *JBTRS*. This text does not mention here sufferings in hell, but it does mention suffering the consequences of sin in many previous births.

In the *Pkp*, it is simply mentioned that as a consequence of his deed, barley was eaten for three months in this last life as Buddha when he was dwelling in Verajjā, having been invited by a Brahman.

---

222. Nalinaksha Dutt, 1947, pp. 4–5.

BN and *UP* state that as a result of asking a virtuous monk to eat barley grains out of abundant alms, now in his last birth as Buddha when a Brahman invited him for alms during the rainy season retreat, Māra made him forget the invitation.[223] *BN* and *UP* state further that when Buddha went to Verañjā there was a famine there and he and the 500 monks accompanying him came out of the village not obtaining any food. Then they went to a market fair of 500 horse dealers who came from the province of Uttarāṅga. Each horse dealer offered barley grains sufficient for his own use. On that day, the Buddha and his monks ate that much. During the full three months of the rainy season, the horse dealers continued making that offering in like manner. The two varying explanations given here for the Buddha and his 500 monks having eaten barley for three months are both contained in the Pāli texts, but they do not agree with one another. In what is perhaps typical South Asian fashion, though, they are placed here in juxtaposition to one another.

The Tibetan text, like the *Pkp*, states simply that the Buddha ate barley for three months when staying in Vairambha, having been invited there by a Brahman.[224]

Taishō no. 199 implies that the Buddha as the teacher it mentioned, who uttered bad speech and thereby went to hell was a Brahman, states that by the remaining disadvantageous *kamma* the Buddha himself suffered the anger of a Brahman. The latter invited the Buddha for alms, and let him spend the entire three months chewing barley. This is the only text among those we are considering that introduces anger as a reason why the Brahman who invited the Buddha allowed him to eat barley for three months. But its explanation fits the context. This text does not mention Vairambha. The Chinese text of *Taishō* no.

---

223. The way in which *BN* and *UP* read here, it states that it is the Buddha who forgot the invitation. But perhaps in accord with the Pāli commentaries it should read that the Brahman forgot the invitation because of Māra. See *DPPN*, vol. 2, p. 929, n. 3.

224. Vairambha is the Sanskrit equivalent of Pāli Verajjā, Sinhalese Verañjā. See *BHSGD*, vol. 2, p. 511b, under Vairambhya (also °bha).

197 mentions the state of P'i-Lan (Vairambha). It states that by the remaining disadvantageous *kamma* both the Buddha and the 500 monks—to whom the sermon is being preached—when invited by a Brahman of the state of P'i-Lan had to eat horse barley for ninety days continuously.

The independent account of the Buddha at Vairambha in a section of the Gilgit manuscripts preceding the *Sthaviragāthā* gives more information on the Buddha at Vairambha than the incomplete prose summary. It states that the Buddha reached Vairambha in South Pañcāla where he converted a Brahman who had an aversion towards the Buddhists. The king of Vairambha at the time was a Brahman named Agnidatta. As a matter of courtesy, Agnidatta invited the Buddha to his kingdom and offered him food and other requisites for three months, which the Buddha accepted. He then asked his men to get food ready for the monks and banned his subjects from offering any gifts on the pain of death. The same night the king had a dream which his Brahman ministers interpreted in such a way that he, at their advice, decided to remain completely cut off from the outside world for three months. He could not give any instruction to his men to offer food to the Buddha and his disciples nor to cancel the order banning his subjects from giving any gifts. So the Buddha and his disciples could not procure any food. Fortunately, at that time a trader reached the place with a large caravan and offered the Buddha and his disciples a portion of the barley grains meant for his horses. All the disciples except Śāriputra and Maudgalyāyana agreed to stay with him and live on barley. After passing the rainy season with this kind of food, Ānanda went to see the king to take his leave. On inquiry, the king recognized his blunder, felt repentant and confessed his sin. He was absolved of his sin and was obliged by Buddha by accepting his invitation for one day. The corresponding story as in the Pāli canon, with some variation in details, is given by *DPPN*.[225]

225. *DPPN*, vol. 2, pp. 929–30. For the sources, see p. 930, n. 4.

The *Av-klp* is very brief here, mentioning only that due to the past sin that still lingered in his life, the Buddha tasted the course food made of *kodrava* grain. Again, as before, the text and the interpretations other than that of *JBTRS* mention both *kodrava* and barley. Giuseppe Tucci, on the basis of the Tibetan translation of this text, says that the Buddha in this life, for his earlier sin, had to eat rotten wheat.

In instances in the stories of this *kamma*, points were introduced for internal consistency within the versions. Thus, the Buddha having been a Brahman teacher of 500 students is introduced in *Taishō* no. 197 so as to explain why the Buddha and 500 monks ate barley with him in Vairambha. The Buddha having sinned by having uttered ill-considered speech when he was a teacher in *Taishō* no. 199 agrees with the statement that, in reciprocal fashion, he too had suffered the anger of a Brahman. Two of the 500 students of the Buddha in his former life having not assented to the aspersion of the Buddha Vipaśyin and his monks in the story as in the Gilgit manuscripts' version explains the following statement that Śāriputra and Maudgalyāyana, who were these two monks, therefore did not stay with the Buddha at this time and eat a diet of barley with him. That *Taishō* no. 197 and the version in the Gilgit manuscripts agree in mentioning 500 students of the Buddha in his former life as well as the 500 monks who ate barley for three months with the Buddha, demonstrates again the close relationship of these two texts. *BN* and *UP* also mention the 500 disciples of the Buddha eating barley with him, and to balance this it introduces 500 horse dealers who each offers barley sufficient for his own use each day of the rainy season. This text does not introduce the 500 students into the antecedent action, though, as do the Gilgit manuscripts' version and *Taishō* no. 197.

Pkp would allow as an explanation for the monks together with the Buddha in Verajjā also eating barley, that the Bodhisatta in *Pkp* cursed the disciples of Phussa, in the plural. *Pkp*, though, does not allude to the Buddha's disciples at Verajjā.

Perhaps introducing local color, *BN* and *UP* mention barley as an acceptable food, just not a preferred food. Wheat and barley are staple foods in the Uttarāṅga area from which the horse dealers came, which is also famous for its swift horses and horse dealers.[226] The corresponding Tibetan text, and *Taishō* no. 199 mention that barley is an acceptable food, just not a preferred food. *Taishō* no. 199 even refers to "red barley". In the text as in *Taishō* no. 197, however, it becomes barley for horses which the Buddha in question, together with his monks, is cursed to eat, and which the Buddha and his 500 disciples eat in Vairambha. In the Gilgit manuscripts' version, in the story regarding the antecedent action it is not mentioned that the barley to be eaten is food for horses, but in the story of the stay at Vairambha, agreeing with *Taishō* no. 197, the trader who reaches Vairambha with a large caravan offers the Buddha and his disciples barley grains meant for his horses. The *Av-klp*, on the contrary, mentions only that the citizens are told Buddhist monks did not have a taste for delicious food, but should be served old *kodrava* and barley grain. That the grain they are to be served is old suggests leftovers, not necessarily food for horses. Also, the Buddha is made to state that in this life he tasted the course food made of *kodrava* and barley grain (*bhunktādya kodravayavāhāraḥ*) suggesting by this interpretation that it was not only grain he was given but prepared food as well. Kṣemendra, of course, was writing in Kashmir where wheat and barley are staples. In this instance, the *Av-klp* does not agree, as if often does, with the Gilgit manuscripts' version or the version in *Taishō* no. 197.

Also possibly demonstrating the inclusion of local color, the Gilgit manuscripts' account of the story refers to a trader and his caravan, suggesting perhaps reference to ancient trade routes such as the Silk Road. Gilgit was on such a trade route. Merchant caravans and caravan guards and guides, of course, are mentioned generally in Pāli literature as well. They are not mentioned, though, in connection with this story.

226. Uttarāṅga, or Uttarapatha, included Kashmir, Gandhāra, and Kamboja.

C. Slandering [the Buddha Kassapa]

The third, and last story we will consider here is that of Jotipāla's slander of the Buddha Kassapa (Skt. Kāśyapa), which is linked with the Buddha's difficulty in obtaining enlightenment in this life.

The *Pkp* notes only that Jotipāla slandered the *sugata* Kassapa, questioning whether a bald-headed ascetic could achieve the enlightenment that is highest and hard to obtain.

BN and *UP* expand on this, indicating that Jotipāla was a Brahman, and that he denied the existence of a Buddha in his day to his potter friend Ghaṭīkāra. He heard of Kāśyapa for the first time from Ghaṭīkāra, and did not believe his friend's words. Dialogue is recounted in full. Emphasis is placed on Jotipāla's opinion that true enlightenment is so rare, that it is unlikely to have occurred in his time. The opinion here that enlightenment is rare reflects the usage of *dullabhā* "difficult to obtain, rare" in the *Pkp* to describe enlightenment.

This is the only story of an antecedent *kamma* in the *Pkp* that is mentioned elsewhere in the Pāli canon.[227] In these other locations, Jotipāla realized his friend's earnestness, and accompanied him eventually to hear Kassapa Buddha preach. Jotipāla then became a monk. It can be noted that not only do *BN* and *UP* expand on *Pkp*, but they also expand on the part of the story elsewhere in the Pāli canon in which Jotipāla at first does not believe his friend's words, and on Ghaṭīkāra's early words to Jotipāla.

In the corresponding Tibetan text, the Sanskrit name corresponding to Jotipāla in the Pāli and Sinhalese texts, Nandipāla, is given as the person to whom the slander is made. The name of the person to whom the slander is made in the Sinhalese texts, and elsewhere in the Pāli canon, Ghaṭīkāra, is also given. But the Tibetan text here misinterprets it as an occupation title, and would have it that the slander was made to Nandipāla when the Buddha in an earlier life had become a potter. The name of the Buddha in question is not given. He is

227. See *DPPN*, vol. 1, p. 971 for references.

referred to only as a "baldhead", or ascetic. The full narration with the names given properly, Nandipāla speaking to Ghaṭīkāra, is given in the *Nandipāla Sūtra* of the *Madhyamāgama*, which corresponds to the *Ghaṭīkāra Sutta* of the *Majjhima Nikāya*. In the Tibetan text the slanderer questions why it should be good for him to go to see the baldheaded ascetic. And he denies that this one has enlightenment.

Among the Chinese texts, *Taishō* no. 199 refers to the Buddha in his previous birth as Nan-t'i-ho-lo (Nandipāla), and the slandered Buddha as Chia-shê (Kāśyapa). It is only *Taishō* no. 199 and the Pāli *Pkp* and Sinhalese *BN* and *UP* that mention the name of the Buddha in question here. And like the *Pkp*, *Taishō* no. 199 does not mention Ghaṭīkāra. The slander itself is very similar in both the Tibetan text and *Taishō* no. 199. *Taishō* no. 199, though, refers to the slandered Buddha as an ascetic (Skt. *śramaṇa*), not a "baldhead" as in the Tibetan text and the *Pkp*, which usage implies an ascetic.

In *Taishō* no. 197, the name of the person to whom the slander is spoken is Hu-hsi (Nandipāla). This is one of the few instances in which *Taishō* no. 197 stands nearer to the Tibetan translation than *Taishō* no. 199.[228] The name of the person by whom the slander is spoken is given here as the lad Huo-men, for which the Sanskrit equivalent is uncertain. The slander, or ill-considered speech, itself is very similar to the *Pkp*. As in the Tibetan text as well, there is mention of one with a shaved head. It then goes on to state, though, not that he has not attained enlightenment or the Buddha-path, but that the Buddha-path is very difficult to follow. This reflects the characterization of enlightenment as "difficult to obtain (*dullabhā*)" in the *Pkp*, as also reflected in *BN* and *UP*, noted above.

Thus, *Taishō* no. 199 starts off being closer to *Pkp* than *Taishō* no. 197, but in the slander itself it stands closer to the Tibetan translation as is more usual. *Taishō* no. 197, on the other hand, starts off being closer to the Tibetan text, but in the slander itself it stands closer to *Pkp*.

---

228. See *AS*, p. 239, n. 2.

The reference to the prose retelling in the Gilgit manuscripts given by Nalinaksha Dutt explains why the Tibetan text had construed Ghaṭīkāra to be an occupation title. Nandipāla is referred to here as Nandipāla Ghaṭīkāra. Dutt, though, refers the reader to the *Madhyamāgama* for the story.[229]

The text of *Av-klp* is aberrant. It would have a man named Uttara speaking ill (Skt. *apavāda*) of one Puṅgala (thus the text). Because of the name or word *puṅgala*, or *puṃgala*, which is a variant of *pudgala*, the interpretations here have been various.

In the reading "Puṅgala" of the text here, "ṅ" for "ṃ" involves changing the nasal to the nasal of the class of the following consonant. Such is common, and vice versa. *BHSGD* translates *pudgala*, which it notes is often written *puṃgala*, "person, man, creature, soul (often = *ātman*)."[230] The interpretation of É. Senart, though, of *pudgala* in *Mvst* 1.85.10 and 1.88.12, 14 is it is to be observed "the great personage (*i.e.* the Buddha)".[231] Edgerton finds this interpretation doubtful. The usage here, though, suggests Senart's interpretation, except here Puṅgala would refer to Kāśyapa Buddha. Also consonant with this is the interpretation of Giuseppe Tucci of the Tibetan text of this passage as referring to the insult being made by Uttara to the Buddha of his time. J. J. Jones translates *pudgala* here as "Foremost Man", construing the usage to imply *agrapudgala* as appears in *Mahāvastu* 1.47.2, and which he notes there to be an appellation of the Buddha practically equivalent to *agrapuruṣa*.[232] Also consider that Edgerton mentions that another reading for *puṃgala* in *Mvst* manuscripts is *puṃgava*, a Sanskrit word that may have influenced the form with nasal, *puṃgala*. Skt. *puṃgava* is used to mean "a bull; a hero, eminent person, chief of (ifc.)".[233] This again, supports Senart's interpretation and the interpretation here.

229. Nalinaksha Dutt, 1947, p. 29.

230. *BHSGD*, p. 347a.

231. This is mentioned in a note on pp. xxviii–xxix in the introduction to vol. 1 of *Mvst*, referred to by *BHSGD*, p. 347a.

232. See J. J. Jones, 1949–56, vol. 1, p. 66, including n. 4, and p.69; and vol. 1, p. 39, n. 4.

233. *MW*, p. 630c.

The slander itself is not mentioned in the *Av-klp*.

Pkp states that as a result of this slander, the Buddha practiced with much difficulty and austerity in Uruvelā. Only then, after six years, did he attain enlightenment. Note in this regard how the two segments of the *Pkp* story here are perfectly balanced in terms of cause and effect. This is not so in any of the other versions. Buddha in a previous life said true enlightenment is hard to attain. In his last life as Buddha, he had difficulty in achieving enlightenment.

BN and *UP* expand on this and explain it more clearly. Due to the Buddha's saying in his earlier life, through ignorance, that the Buddha Kāśyapa was not a Buddha, now in this birth he has found it difficult to obtain Buddhahood. Whereas other Buddhas became such after seven days or a few months after their renunciation, he became Buddha only after a full six years of exertion in the province of Uruvelā.

The Tibetan text states that when the Buddha reached human existence again and wandered as a mendicant with the desire for the highest enlightenment, he went through the course of difficult tasks engaged in by a Bodhisatta (Skt. *duṣkaracaryā*) for six years in Uruvelā, and thereby endured much suffering. Skt. *duṣkaracaryā* here corresponds to Pāli *ācariṃ dukkaraṃ bahuṃ* in the *Pkp*.

Taishō no. 199 does not give parallel text here. *Taishō* no. 197, though, states in lengthy fashion that because of this bad *kamma* the Buddha took six years to the day in the way of life of religious castigation of himself in the hope that the path of the Buddha could be completed. He could not, though, complete the path of the Buddha through this way of life in self-castigation. He went, on account of his *karma*, on a false way in his search.

In this location, there is a partial preservation of a verse from the Turfan manuscripts. As far as this can be made out, it states that the Buddha went through great suffering and difficult tasks as a result of his former deeds (of heroic energy) during six years in Uruvelā.

Nalinaksha Dutt states here that the purpose of the story here is to explain why the Buddha had to undergo extreme self-mortification for six years before the attainment of enlightenment.[234] This explanation resembles the initial statement of *Taishō* no. 197, the close relationship with this manuscript has been mentioned a number of times. We cannot be sure here, though, whether this is Dutt's opinion or fact.

The *Av-klp* adds a twist in this location. It states that the Buddha had to undergo hardship for six years due to his previous evil deeds. But then it adds that he did not obtain any food to eat during this time. This statement about difficulty in obtaining alms is probably added for reasons of balance in the structure of the text.

---

234. Nalinaksha Dutt, 1947, p. 29.

Conclusion

There remain two desiderata regarding this text.

One is a translation of *Ap-a*. As occurred in the Northern Buddhist tradition, the order of the stories of *Pkp* is also changed here. The difference is that here the order is changed so that the stories are chronological in terms of the Buddha's present life, this being just one way in which the author attempted to respond to denials that the Buddha experienced bad *kamma*. It is, though, like the reordering of the text in the Northern Buddhist tradition, an attempt to find a more comprehensible organization of the text.

A second desideratum is a defensible translation of the *Av-klp*. The variations in the various interpretations of the text are uncalled for. There is not even agreement on the spellings of many proper names.

Enough details are similar between the Pāli and Sinhalese material, the Sarvāstivāda and Mūlasarvāstivāda material, and the Mahāyāna material to indicate that we clearly have one tradition. While this is not always the case, among the Northern Buddhist versions, the Tibetan version and the version as in *Taishō* no. 199 agree more closely with one another. The version in *Taishō* no. 197 often agrees with the version reflected in the Gilgit manuscripts' incomplete prose recounting and with the version of the *Av-klp*, the latter two of which agree closely enough with one another that we can refer to them as a Kashmiri recension. Both versions hail from Kashmir. The Pāli *Pkp* is generally close to the Tibetan version, though the *Pkp* version contains more *kammas*. Occasionally *Taishō* no. 197 agrees with the *Pkp* version as against *Taishō* no. 199, just as *Taishō* no. 197 occasionally agrees with the Tibetan version over *Taishō* no. 199. The Sinhalese *UP* and *BN*, which expand on the Pali *Pkp*, sometimes agree with the Chinese *Taishō* no. 197, and with the version represented in the Gilgit manuscripts' incomplete prose retelling and the *Av-klp* version, but on the whole they are separate from that subtradition.

That the tradition points to the discourse as having been given at Anotatta (Skt. Anavatapta) Lake throughout, and as the Mahāyāna tradition relates at the beginning of the text an incident from the beginning of the *Sthaviragāthā*,[235] suggests that the tradition has a Sarvāstivāda and Mūlasarvāstivāda origin, or perhaps more generally a Sanskrit Hīnayāna origin when we consider the parallel story in the Mahāsaṅghika *Mahāvastu-avadāna* to the slander by the Bodhisatta of a disciple of the Buddha Sabbābhibhū, and the resulting slander of the Buddha by a woman. But as has been noted here, it seems likely on the basis of organizational considerations, among others, that the stories preserved in the textual tradition of the Pāli *Pkp*, which are not included in the extant Northern Buddhist versions of the text, are original.

There is evidence in both the Southern Buddhist tradition and the Northern Buddhist tradition that there has been a contraction of the text, followed by an expansion. The way in which the tradition was contracted and expanded, though, differed in the Southern and Northern Buddhist traditions. The Southern Buddhist Pāli tradition of the *Pkp* shortened the text to thirty-two verses, not counting the verse containing the final summation. The significance of this number to the tradition is emphasized in the titles of *UP* and *BN*. This shortening of the text of *Pkp* would seem to have removed verses for some of the *kamma*s that we find evidence of in the Tibetan version. The Northern Buddhist tradition shortened the text to ten *kammas*. The Southern Buddhist Sinhalese tradition of *UP* and *BN* subsequently expanded the tradition by relating the *kamma*s more fully and by increasing the number of *kamma*s recounted, adding new *kamma*s in a balanced fashion that agreed with the organization of *Pkp*. The Northern Buddhist

235. See Marcel Hofinger, 1954, pp. 181–84, p. 190.

tradition also in some cases related some of the *kammas* more fully and with additional details, as in the *Av-klp*. In some cases it also expanded the tradition by substituting a different *kamma* for an established *kamma*, or by including a different antecedent story. The former may have been the case in the Turfan manuscripts' text (we cannot be sure since we have so little of the text), and was the case in the *Av-klp*. In the instance of the *Av-klp* the presently edited text leaves a very brief and incomplete remnant of a *kamma* omitted as well. In other instances, it substituted just a variation of a routinely related *kamma*, as is the case in the Gilgit manuscripts' incomplete prose retelling and in the *Av-klp*. Once the number of *kammas* was set at ten in the Northern Buddhist tradition, this appears never to have changed.

There appears as well to have been instability in the Northern Buddhist tradition regarding the ordering of the stories once their balanced organization as represented in *Pkp* was altered. This is reflected especially in the subtradition represented by the Gilgit manuscripts' incomplete prose retelling of the text and the *Av-klp*, determined here to be a distinct Kashmiri recension.

It is hoped that the presentation of *BN* and *UP* here, and of the various interpretations of the text as in chapter 50 of the *Av-klp* juxtaposed to one another, as well as the discussion and comparison of stories in various versions of the text, have added to our understanding of this textual tradition.

Abbreviations

Ap *The Apadāna of the Khuddaka Nikāya, Part I, edited by Mary E. Lilley. London: Oxford University Press for The Pali Text Society, 1925.*

Ap-a *Visuddhajanavilāsinī nāma Apadānaṭṭhakathā, edited by C. E. Godakumbura. London: Luzac and Company, Ltd. for The Pali Text Society, 1954.*

Ap S *Apadāna Pāli, with the Sinhala Translation, Parts I–II (1–2), by Venerable Pandita Talalle Dhammananda Thera. Buddha Jayanti Tripitaka Series 36–37 (1–2). [Colombo]: Published under the Patronage of the Government of Ceylon, 1961–83. [Part II (2) translated by Pandit Wendaruwe Siri Anomadassi Thera.]*

AS *Bruchstücke buddhistischer Verssammlungen aus zentralasiatischen Sanskrithandschriften. 1, Die Anavataptagāthā und die Sthaviragāthā, by Heinz Bechert. Sanskrittexte aus den Turfanfunden 6. Deutsche Akademie der Wissenschaften zu Berlin, Institute für Orientforschung, Veröffentlichung 51. Berlin: Akademie Verlag, 1961.*

Av-klp *Bodhisattvāvadānakalpalatā, by Kṣemendra. Edition edited by Sarat Chandra Das and Paṇḍit Hari Mohan Vidyābhūshaṇa published under the title, Avadāna Kalpalatā, A Collection of Legendary Stories About the Bodhisattvas, by Kshemendra, with its Tibetan Version ..., 2 vols. Bibliotheca Indica [124]. Calcutta: W. Carey at the Baptist Mission Press and Asiatic Society of Bengal, 1888–1918. Sanskrit text of chapter 50 published as well in JBTRS 1.4, 1893, pp. 9–20 of Sanskrit text section.*

Av-ś *Avadānaçataka: A Century of Edifying Tales belonging to the Hīnayāna, 2 vols., edited by J. S. Speyer. Bibliotheca*

Buddhica 3. St. Petersbourg: Commissionnaires de l'Académie Impériale des Sciences, 1902–1909.

Bhes *Bhesajjamañjūsā, Chapters 1–18, edited by J. Liyanaratne. Oxford: The Pali Text Society, 1996.*

BHSGD *Buddhist Hybrid Sanskrit Grammar and Dictionary, 2 vols., by F. Edgerton. 1953; Rpt. Delhi: Motilal Banarsidass, 1970.*

BN *Detiskarmmaya. J. Liyanaratne, 1983, Ms. no. 6 (Smith-Lesouf 269), text no. 68: ff. nau verso, line 7 to phi recto, line 5.*

CM *The Casket of Medicine (Bhesajjamañjūsā, Chapters 1–18), translated by J. Liyanaratne. Pali Text Society Translation Series 50. Oxford: The Pali Text Society, 2002.*

CPD *A Critical Pali Dictionary, begun by V. Trenckner. Vols. 1–3, fasc. 7, edited by Dines Anderson, Helmer Smith, Hans Hendriksen et al. Copenhagen: The Royal Danish Academy of Sciences and Letters; Commissioner, Munksgaard, 1924–2001. Vol. 1 issued in 11 parts, with an Epilegomena by Helmer Smith. Parts 1–4 published by A. F. Host for The Royal Danish Academy; parts 5–10 published by Levin and Munksgaard for The Royal Danish Academy. Vol. 2 issued in 17 parts.*

CS CD-ROM *Chaṭṭha Saṅgāyana CD-Rom, Version 3. Igatpuri 422 403, India: Vipassana Research Institute, [n.d.].*

Dh *The Dhammapada, edited by Sūriyagoḍa Sumaṅgala Thera. London: Published for the Pali Text Society by Humphrey Milford, Oxford University Press, 1914.*

Divy *The Divyâvadâna, A Collection of Early Buddhist Legends, edited by E. B. Cowell and R. A. Neil. 1886; Rpt. Amsterdam: Oriental Press NV and Philo Press, 1970.*

DPPN *Dictionary of Pāli Proper Names, 2 vols., by G. P. Malalasekera. Indian Texts Series. London: John Murray, 1937–38.*

EncBuddh *Encyclopaedia of Buddhism, vols. 1–6, fasc. 4, edited by G. P. Malalasekera et al. [Columbo]: Published by the Government of Ceylon, 1961–2002.*

J — *The Jātaka together with its Commentary, being Tales of the Anterior Births of Gotama Buddha, 7 vols., edited by V. Fausbøll. London: Trübner and Co., 1877–97.*

JBTRS — *Journal of the Buddhist Text and Research Society, Calcutta, edited by Sarat Chandra Das, 1–7, 1893–1906. [1893–96 name of society appears as Buddhist Text Society of India. 1897–1901 name appears as Buddhist Text and Anthropological Society.]*

KS — *The Book of the Kindred Sayings (Saŋyutta-Nikāya) or Grouped Suttas, 5 vols. Pali Text Translation Series 7, 10, 13, 14, 16. Vol. 1, Kindred Sayings with Verses (Sagāthā-Vagga), translated by C. A. F. Rhys Davids, assisted by Sūriyagoḍa Sumaṅgala Thera. Vol. 2, The Nidāna Book (Nidāna-vagga), translated by C. A. F. Rhys Davids, assisted by F. L. Woodward. Vol. 3, [The Khandhā Book (Khandhā-vagga)], Vol. 4, [The Salāyatana Book (Salāyatana-vagga)], Vol. 5, Mahāvagga, translated by F. L. Woodward, edited or with an introduction by C. A. F. Rhys Davids. London: Published for the Pali Text Society by Oxford University Press, [1917]–1930.*

Mahidol U CD-ROM — *Buddhist Scriptures on CD-Rom, MS-DOS Edition. Bangkok, Thailand: Mahidol University Computing Center, © 1994.*

Mvst — *Le Mahâvastu, Texte Sanscrit Publié pour la Première Fois et Accompagné d'Introductions et d'un Commentaire, 3 vols, by É. Senart. Société Asiatique, Collection d'Ouvrages Orientaux, Seconde Série. Paris: L'Imprimerie Nationale, 1882–97.*

MW — *A Sanskrit-English Dictionary, new ed, by M. Monier-Williams. Oxford: The Clarendon Press, 1899.*

PED — *The Pali Text Society's Pali-English Dictionary, by T. W. Rhys Davids and W. Stede. 1921–25; Rpt. London: The Pali Text Society, 1972.*

Pkp — *Pubbakammapiloti of the Apadāna of the Khuddaka Nikāya.*

QKM *The Questions of King Milinda, 2 vols., translated by T. W. Rhys Davids. The Sacred Books of the East 35–36. 1890–94; Rpt. New York: Dover Publications, Inc., 1963.*

S *The Samyutta-Nikâya of the Sutta-Piṭaka, 6 vols., edited by Léon Feer. Vol. 6, Indexes, by C. A. F. Rhys Davids. London: Published for the Pali Text Society, by H. Frowde, 1884–1904.*

SBFB *The Jātaka, or Stories of the Buddha's Former Births, translated from the Pāli by various hands under the editorship of E. B. Cowell, 7 vols. 1895–1913; Rpt. London: The Pali Text Society, 1973.*

Taishō *Taishō shinshū daizōkyō (The Tripitaka in Chinese), 85 vols., edited by Junjirō Takadusu and Kaikyoku Watanabe. 1924–27; Rpt. Tokyo: The Taishō Shinshū Daizōkyō Kanko Kai, [1961–78].*

Ud-a *Paramattha-Dīpanī Udānaṭṭhakathā (Udāna Commentary) of Dhammapālâcariya, edited by F. L. Woodward. London: Oxford University Press for The Pali Text Society, 1926.*

UP *Detiskarma padārthayi. S. H. Levitt, 1980, Ms. no. M27, section K: ff. chṛ recto, line 1 to jṛ recto, line 6.*

Vin *The Vinaya Piṭakam: One of the Principal Buddhist Holy Scriptures in the Pâli Language, 5 vols., edited by H. Oldenberg. 1879–83; Rpt. London: Published for the Pali Text Society by Routledge and Kegan Paul Ltd. (vol. 1, by Luzac and Company, Ltd.), 1969–84.*

VT *Vinaya Texts, 2 vols., translated by T. W. Rhys Davids and H. Oldenberg. The Sacred Books of the East 13 and 17. 1881–82; Rpt. Delhi: Motilal Banarsidass, 1965.*

References

"B." and Pandit Ananda Prasād Sarasvatī. 1893. "Ten Sufferings of Buddha, Translation of the 50th *Pallava* of Kshemendra's Kalpalatā." In *JBTRS* 1.4: 19–25. [Pp. 19–22, translation by "B."; pp. 22–25, translation by Pandit Ananda Prasād Sarasvatī.]

Babbitt, Irving. 1936. *The Dhammapada*. Rpt. New York: New Directions Publishing Corporation, 1965.

Bary, Wm. Theodore de, Stephen N. Hay, Royal Weiler, Andrew Yarrow (eds). 1958. *Sources of Indian Tradition. Introduction to Oriental Civilizations*. New York: Columbia University Press.

Basham, A. L. 1958. "Jainism and Buddhism." In Bary, Wm. Theodore de, Stephen N. Hay, Royal Weiler, Andrew Yarrow (eds), 37–202.

Bechert, Heinz. 1958. "Über das Apadānabuch." In *Wiener Zeitschrift für die Kunde Süd- und Ostasiens und Archiv für Insdische Philosophie* 2: 1–21.

Bechert, Heinz. 1961–65. "Anavataptagāthā." In *EncBuddh*, vol. 1: 796b–97b.

Besant, Annie. 1904. *The Bhagavad-Gita, The Lord's Song. Text in Devanagari and Translation*. 9th ed. Adyar, Madras: The Theosophical Publishing House, 1955.

Brown, W. Norman. 1940–41. "The Basis for the Hindu Act of Truth." In *Review of Religion* 5: 36–45.

Brown, W. Norman. 1972. "Duty as Truth in Ancient India." In *Proceedings of the American Philosophical Society* 116: 252–68. Rpt. in Rosane Rocher (ed.), 102–119.

Burlingame, E. W. 1917. "The Act of Truth (Saccakiriyā): A Hindu Spell and Its Employment as a Psychic Motif in Hindu Fiction." In *Journal of the Royal Asiatic Society of Great Britain and Ireland* [no vol. no.]: 429–67.

Carter, J. R. and M. Palihawadana. 1987. *The Dhammapada.* New York and Oxford: Oxford University Press.

Chalmers, Lord Robert. 1932. *Buddha's Teachings, being the Sutta-Nipāta or Discourse-Collection, Edited in the Original Pāli Text with an English Version Facing It. Harvard Oriental Series* 37. Cambridge, Massachusetts: Harvard University Press.

Chattopadhyay, Jayanti. 1994. *Bodhisattva Avadānakalpalatā, A Critical Study.* Calcutta: Atisha Memorial Publishing Society; copies available from Sanskrit Pustak Bhandar.

Cutler, S. M. 1994. "The Pāli Apadāna Collection." In *Journal of the Pali Text Society* 20: 1–42.

Das, Nobin Chandra. 1895. *Legends and Miracles of Buddha, Sakya Sinha, Part I, Translated from the Avadan Kalpalata of Bodhi-Sattwas of the Great Sanskrit Poet Kshemendra.* Calcutta: Jadu Nath Seal, Hare Press.

Dutt, Nalinaksha. 1947. *Gilgit Manuscripts*, vol. 3, part 1. 2nd ed. Delhi: Sri Satguru Publications, 1984.

Edgerton, F. 1944. *The Bhagavad Gītā*, 2 vols. *Harvard Oriental Series* 38 and 39. Cambridge, Massachusetts: Harvard University Press. Rpt. of preface, translation, and notes to the translation, with some revisions, New York: Harper Torchbooks, 1964.

Feer, Léon. 1897. "Cinca-Mânavikâ Sundarî." In *Journal Asiatique* n.s. 9: 288–317.

Garfield, Jay L. 1995. *The Fundamental Wisdom of the Middle Way, Nāgārjuna's Mūlamadhyamakārikā.* New York and Oxford: Oxford University Press.

Hofinger, Marcel. 1954. *Le Congres du Lac Anavatapta (Vies de Saints Bouddhiques), Extrait du Vinayades Mūlasarvāstivādin,*

Bhaiṣajyavastu. I. *Légendes des Anciens (Sthavirāvadāna)*. *Bibliothèque du Muséon* 34. Louvain: Publications Universitaires et Institut orientaliste, 1954.

Jones, J. J. 1949–56. *The Mahāvastu*, 3 vols. *Sacred Books of the Buddhists* 16, 18, 19. London: Luzac and Company, Ltd.

Kirfel, W. 1920. *Die Kosmographie der Inder, nach den Quellen dargestellt*. Bonn: Kurt Schroeder.

Lamotte, É. 1949. *Le Traité de la Grande Vertu de Sagesse de Nāgārjuna (Mahāprajñāpāramitāśāstra)*, tome II (Chapitres XVI–XXX). *Bibliothèque du Muséon* 18. Rpt. *Publications de l'Institut Orientaliste de Louvain* 26. Louvain-la-Neuve: Université de Louvain, Institut orientaliste, 1981.

Lamotte, É. 1988. *History of Indian Buddhism, from the Origins to the Śaka Era*, translated from the French by Sara Webb-Boin under the supervision of Jean Dantinne. *Publications de l'Institut Orientaliste de Louvain* 36. Louvain-la-Neuve: Université Catholique de Louvain, Institut orientaliste. (Original: 1958.)

Levitt, S. H. 1980. *A Descriptive Catalogue of the Indic and Greater Indic Manuscripts in the Collection of the University Museum of the University of Pennsylvania*. In *The Library Chronicle* 44.2: 97–152, 10 plates.

Levitt, S. H. 2003. "The Dating of the Indian Tradition." In *Anthropos* 98.2: 341–59.

Ling, T. O. 1972. *A Dictionary of Buddhism: A Guide to Thought and Tradition*. New York: Charles Scribner's Sons.

Liyanaratne, J. 1983. *Bibliothèque Nationale, Départment des Manuscrits, Catalogue des Manuscrits Singhalais*. Paris: Bibliothèque Nationale.

Liyanaratne, J. 1999. *Buddhism and Traditional Medicine in Sri Lanka*. *Kelaniya University Anniversary Series* 1. Kelaniya: Kelaniya University Press.

Mitra, Rājendralāla. 1882. *The Sanskrit Buddhist Literature of Nepal*. Rpt. Calcutta: Sanskrit Pustak Bhandar, 1971.

Müller, F. Max. 2000. *Wisdom of the Buddha: The Unabridged Dhammapada* [with new introductory note and explanatory footnotes]. Mineola, New York: Dover Publications, Inc. (1st ed. New York, 1900.)

Narada Thera. 1954. *The Dhammapada*. Rpt. London: John Murray, 1959.

Norman, K. R. 1983. *Pāli Literature, including the Canonical Literature in Prakrit and Sanskrit of all the Hīnayāna Schools of Buddhism. A History of Indian Literature* 7.2. Wiesbaden: Otto Harrassowitz.

Nyanatiloka. [1970?] *Buddhist Dictionary: Manual of Buddhist Terms and Doctrines*, 3rd rev. and enl. ed. by Nyanaponika. Rpt. Singapore: Singapore Buddhist Meditation Centre, [1987?]. (1st ed., [1946?].)

Perera, H. R. 1966. "Apadāna." In *EncBuddh*, vol. 2: 2a–3b.

Rachlin, Harvey. 2000. *Jumbo's Hide, Elvis's Ride, and the Tooth of Buddha: More Marvelous Tales of Historical Artifacts*. New York: Henry Holt and Company.

Radhakrishnan, Sarvepalli and Charles A. Moore (eds). 1957. *A Sourcebook in Indian Philosophy*. 5th Princeton paperback printing, Princeton, New Jersey: Princeton University Press, 1973.

Rani, Sharada. 1977. *Buddhist Tales of Kashmir in Tibetan Woodcuts (Narthang Series of the Woodcuts of Ksemendra's Avadana-kalpalata)*. *Śata-Pitaka Series, Indo-Asian Literatures* 232. New Delhi: Mrs. Sharada Rani.

Rocher, Rosane (ed.). 1978. *India and Indology: Selected Articles by W. Norman Brown*. Delhi: Motilal Banarsidass.

Salomon, Richard. 1999. *Ancient Buddhist Scrolls from Gandhāra: The British Library Kharoṣṭhī Fragments*. Seattle: University of Washington Press.

Salomon, Richard. 2003. "The Senior Manuscripts: Another Collection of Gandhāran Buddhist Scrolls." In *Journal of the American Oriental Society* 123.1: 73–92.

Skorupski, Tadeusz. 2002. *The Six Perfections: An Abridged Version of E. Lamotte's French Translation of Nāgārjuna's Mahāprajñāpāramitāśāstra, Chapters XVI-XXX. Buddhica Britannica, Series Continua* 9. Tring, U.K.: The Institute of Buddhist Studies.

Somadasa, K. D. 1959–64. *Lāṅkāvē Puskoḷa Pot Nāmāvaḷiya*, I–II.Colombo: Department of Cultural Affairs, Government of Sri Lanka.

Tucci, Giuseppe. 1949. *Tibetan Painted Scrolls*, 3 vols. Rpt. Bangkok, Thailand: SDI Publications, ©1999 by Bruce L. Miller.

Walters, J. S. 1990. "The Buddha's Bad Karma: A Problem in the History of Theravâda Buddhism." In *Numen* 37.1: 70–95.

Yamaguchi, Susumu. 1927. "Nāgārjuna's *Mahāyāna Viṁśaka*." In *The Eastern Buddhist* 4.2: 169–71. Rpt. in Sarvepalli Radhakrishnan and Charles A. Moore (eds.), 338–39.

ABOUT PARIYATTI

Pariyatti is dedicated to providing affordable access to authentic teachings of the Buddha about the Dhamma theory (*pariyatti*) and practice (*paṭipatti*) of Vipassana meditation. A 501(c)(3) nonprofit charitable organization since 2002, Pariyatti is sustained by contributions from individuals who appreciate and want to share the incalculable value of the Dhamma teachings. We invite you to visit www.pariyatti.org to learn about our programs, services, and ways to support publishing and other undertakings.

Pariyatti Publishing Imprints

Vipassana Research Publications (focus on Vipassana as taught by S.N. Goenka in the tradition of Sayagyi U Ba Khin)

BPS Pariyatti Editions (selected titles from the Buddhist Publication Society, copublished by Pariyatti)

MPA Pariyatti Editions (selected titles from the Myanmar Pitaka Association, copublished by Pariyatti)

Pariyatti Digital Editions (audio and video titles, including discourses)

Pariyatti Press (classic titles returned to print and inspirational writing by contemporary authors)

Pariyatti enriches the world by

- disseminating the words of the Buddha,
- providing sustenance for the seeker's journey,
- illuminating the meditator's path.

www.ingramcontent.com/pod-product-compliance
Lightning Source LLC
Chambersburg PA
CBHW031555040426
42452CB00006B/314
* 9 7 8 1 6 8 1 7 2 4 6 4 5 *